SIX MEMOS

FOR THE NEXT MILLENNIUM

1 - Lightness
2 - Quickness
3 - Exactitude
4 - Visibility
5 - Multiplicity
6 - Consistency

Six Memos for the Next Millennium

BOOKS BY ITALO CALVINO

ITALO CALVINO

Six Memos for the Next Millennium

A new translation from the Italian by GEOFFREY BROCK

 MARINER CLASSICS

New York   Boston

First Mariner Books edition 2016

Mariner Books
An Imprint of HarperCollins Publishers, registered
in the United States of America and / or other jurisdictions.

www.marinerbooks.com

First published in Italy as *Lezioni americane,* by Garzanti Libri, Milan, 1988.
First published in the United States (in a translation by Patrick Creagh)
by Harvard University Press in 1988 and subsequently by Vintage Books,
a division of Penguin Random House, in 1993.

Library of Congress Cataloging-in-Publication Data
Names: Calvino, Italo, author. | Brock, Geoffrey, date, translator.
Title: Six memos for the next millennium / Italo Calvino ; a new translation
Description: Boston : Mariner Books, 2016
Identifiers: LCCN 2016008858 (print) | LCCN 2016020898 (ebook) | ISBN
9780544146679 (paperback) | ISBN 9780544230965 (ebook)
Subjects: LCSH: Literature — Philosophy. | Style, Literary. |
Literature — History and criticism. | BISAC: LITERARY CRITICISM / General.
| LITERARY CRITICISM / Books & Reading.
Classification: LCC PN45 .C33213 2016 (print) | LCC PN45 (ebook) | DDC
801 — dc23
LC record available at https: / / lccn.loc.gov / 2016008858

Printed in the United States of America
23 24 25 26 27 LBC 14 13 12 11 10

Frontispiece courtesy of the Estate of Italo Calvino.

Grateful acknowledgment is made for permission to quote from the follow-
ing: "Piccolo Testamento" from *La bufera e altro* by Eugenio Montale, reprinted by permission of Mondadori Libri S.p.A. *Quer pasticciaccio brutto de
Via Merulana* by Carlo Emilio Gadda, reprinted by permission of Garzanti
Libri S.r.l, a division of Gruppo editoriale Mauri Spagnol, and by permission
of the Estate of Carlo Emilio Gadda. "A sepal, petal, and a thorn" from
The Poems of Emily Dickinson, edited by Ralph W. Franklin, Cambridge,
Mass.: The Belknap Press of Harvard University Press, copyright © 1998,
1999 by the President and Fellows of Harvard College, copyright © 1951,
1955 by the President and Fellows of Harvard College, copyright © renewed
1979, 1983 by the President and Fellows of Harvard College, copyright ©
1914, 1918, 1919, 1924, 1929, 1930, 1932, 1935, 1937, 1942 by Martha Dickinson
Bianchi, copyright © 1952, 1957, 1958, 1963, 1965 by Mary L. Hampson.

Note on the Text

On June 6, 1984, Italo Calvino was officially invited by Harvard University to give the Charles Eliot Norton Poetry Lectures, a series of six talks meant to take place over the course of an academic year. (For Calvino, it was to have been 1985–1986.) The term *poetry* here refers to any type of poetic communication—literary, musical, visual—and the choice of topic is entirely free.

That freedom was the first problem Calvino faced, convinced as he was of the importance of constraints in writing. By January 1985 he had clearly defined his topic—certain literary values to recommend to the next millennium—and from that point on he devoted nearly all his time to preparing these talks. They soon became an obsession, and one day he told me he had ideas and material for at least eight lectures, not just the expected six. I know the title of what might have been the eighth: "On Beginning and Ending" (with regard to novels), but I have yet to find a draft—only notes.

By September 1985, the time of his scheduled departure for Massachusetts, he had written five of the lectures. The sixth, "Consistency" — of which I know only that he planned to refer to Melville's "Bartleby" — was to have been written in Cambridge.

Of course, these are the talks Calvino would have delivered orally; they would certainly have been revised again prior to publication. I don't think, however, that he would have made significant changes. The differences between the first versions I saw and the last had to do with structure, not content.

About the title: Although I carefully considered the fact that the title he chose, "Six Memos for the Next Millennium," does not correspond to the manuscript as I found it, I have felt it necessary to keep it. He was delighted by the word *memos,* having thought of and dismissed titles such as "Some Literary Values," "A Choice of Literary Values," "Six Literary Legacies" — all followed by "for the Next Millennium."

I'll add only that I found the typescript on his desk, in perfect order, each individual talk in its own transparent folder, ready to be placed in his suitcase.

Esther Calvino

Contents

Six Memos for the Next Millennium

It's 1985: just fifteen years separate us from the beginning of a new millennium. For now the approach of this date does not stir in me any particular emotion. In any case I am here to speak not of futurology but of literature. The millennium that is winding down has seen the birth and spread of the modern languages of the West and the literatures that have explored the expressive, cognitive, and imaginative possibilities of these languages. It was also the millennium of the book, in that it saw the book-object take the form we know it by today. Perhaps one sign that the millennium is winding down is the frequency with which the fate of literature and the book in the so-called postindustrial age is being questioned. I'm not inclined to weigh in on such matters. My faith in the future of literature rests on the knowledge that there are things that only literature, with its particular capacities, can give us. I would like then to devote these talks of mine to certain values or qualities or peculiarities of literature that are especially close to my heart, in an effort to situate them with a view to the new millennium.

I

Lightness

I will devote my first talk to the opposition between lightness and weight, and I will make the case for lightness. This is not to say that I regard the case for weight as weaker, only that I think I have more to say about lightness.

After four decades of writing fiction, after exploring many avenues and undertaking various experiments, the time has come for me to seek a general definition of my work. I propose this one: my method has entailed, more often than not, the subtraction of weight. I have tried to remove weight from human figures, from celestial bodies, from cities. Above all I have tried to remove weight from the structure of the story and from language.

In this talk I will try to explain—to myself as well as to you—why I have come to regard lightness as a virtue rather than a fault, where among the works of the past I find examples of my ideal of lightness, and how I locate this quality in the present and project it into the future.

• • •

I'll start with the last point. When I began my career, the duty of every young writer, the categorical imperative, was to represent our times. Full of good intentions, I tried to become one with the ruthless energy that, collectively and individually, was driving the events of our century. I tried to find some harmony between the bustling spectacle of the world, by turns dramatic and grotesque, and the picaresque, adventurous inner rhythm that spurred me to write. I soon realized that the gap between the realities of life that were supposed to be my raw materials and the sharp, darting nimbleness that I wanted to animate my writing was becoming harder and harder for me to bridge. Perhaps I was only then becoming aware of the heaviness, the inertia, the opacity of the world—qualities that quickly adhere to writing if one doesn't find a way to give them the slip.

I sometimes felt that the whole world was turning to stone: a slow petrifaction, more advanced in some people and places than in others, but from which no aspect of life was spared. It was as if no one could escape Medusa's inexorable gaze.

The only hero capable of cutting off Medusa's head is Perseus, who flies on winged sandals, Perseus, who looks not upon the Gorgon's face but only upon her image reflected in his bronze shield. And so it is that Perseus comes to my aid even now, as I begin to feel caught in a grip of stone, as happens whenever I try to mix the historical and the autobiographical. Better to make my argument using images from mythology. In order to cut off Medusa's head without being turned to stone, Perseus supports himself on the lightest of stuff — wind and clouds — and turns his gaze toward that which can be revealed to him only indirectly, by an image caught in a mirror. I am immediately tempted to find in this myth an allegory of the relationship between the poet and the world, a lesson about how to write. But I know that every interpretation of a myth impoverishes and suffocates it; with myths, it's better not to rush things, better to let them settle in memory, pausing to consider their details, to ponder them without moving beyond the language of their images. The lesson we can draw from a myth lies within the literality of its story, not in what we add to it from without.

The relationship between Perseus and the Gorgon is complex, and it doesn't end with the beheading of the monster. From Medusa's blood a winged horse, Pegasus, is born; the heaviness of stone is transformed into its opposite, and with the stamp of a single hoof on Mount Helicon, a fountain springs forth from which the Muses drink. In some versions of the myth, it is Perseus who rides this marvelous horse, so dear to the Muses, born from the cursed blood of Medusa. (The winged sandals, by the way, also come from the world of monsters: Perseus got them from Medusa's sisters, the Graeae, who shared a single eye.) As for the severed head, rather than abandoning it, Perseus takes it with him, hidden in a sack. When in danger of defeat, he has only to show it to his enemies, lifting it by its mane of snakes, and in the hero's hand the bloody prize becomes an invincible weapon — a weapon he uses only in dire need and only against those who deserve the punishment of being turned into statues of themselves. Here, certainly, the myth is telling me something, something that is implicit in its images and can't be explained by other means. Perseus masters that terrible face by keeping it hidden, just as he had earlier defeated it by looking at its reflection. In each case his power derives from refusing to look directly while not denying the reality of the world of monsters in which he must live, a reality he carries with him and bears as his personal burden.

We can learn more about the relationship between Perseus and Medusa by reading Ovid's *Metamorphoses*. Perseus has won another battle, has hacked a sea monster to death with his sword, freeing Andromeda. And now he wants to do what any of us would do after such a nasty job: he wants to wash his hands. At such times he must decide what to do with Medusa's head. And here I find Ovid's verses (IV, 740–752) extraordinary for the way they show how much delicacy of spirit is required to be a Perseus, a slayer of monsters: "That the rough sand not harm the snake-haired head [*anguiferumque caput dura ne laedat harena*], he makes the ground soft with a bed of leaves, and over that spreads sprigs that grew in water, and there he sets Medusa's head, face-down." I can think of no better way to represent the lightness of which Perseus is the hero than with his refreshingly tender gesture toward that being who, though monstrous and terrifying, is also somehow perishable, fragile. But the most surprising part is the miracle that follows: when the marine plants come into contact with Medusa, they are transformed into coral, and the nymphs, wanting to adorn themselves with coral, rush to bring more sprigs and seaweed to the terrible head.

Again, this juxtaposition of images, in which the delicate grace of the coral brushes up against the fierce horror of the Gorgon, is so richly suggestive that I hesitate to spoil it with commentary or interpretation. What I can do is place these lines of Ovid alongside those of a modern poet, Eugenio Montale, in whose 1953 poem "Piccolo testamento" ("Little Testament") we also find the subtlest of elements, which could stand as emblems of his poetry — "mother-of-pearl snail's track / or emery of trampled glass" (*traccia madreperlacea di lumaca / o smeriglio di vetro calpestato*) — set against a frightening infernal monster, a Lucifer with wings of pitch descending on the capitals of the West. Nowhere else does Montale conjure such an apocalyptic vision, and yet what he foregrounds are those tiny, luminous traces that counterpoint the dark catastrophe: "Keep its powder in your compact / when after every lamp's gone out / the circle dance becomes infernal" (*Conservane la cipria nello specchietto / quando spenta ogni lampada / la sardana si farà infernale*). But how can we hope to find salvation in that which is most fragile? Montale's poem is a profession of faith in the perseverance of what seems most doomed to perish, and in the moral values that imbue the faintest traces: "the faint flare down below / was not the striking of a match" (*il tenue bagliore strofinato / laggiù non era quello d'un fiammifero*).

And so it is that in order to speak of our own times, I have had to make a long detour, by way of Ovid's fragile Medusa and Montale's pitch-black Lucifer. It's hard for a novelist to convey his idea of lightness with examples drawn from the events of contemporary life without making it the unattainable object of an endless quest. Yet Milan Kundera has done just that, with clarity and immediacy. His novel *Nesnesitelná lehkost bytí* (*The Unbearable Lightness of Being*, 1981) is in fact a bitter declaration of the Ineluctable Weight of Living—living not only with the desperate and all-pervading state of oppression that was the fate of his unlucky country, but with the human condition shared also by us, however much luckier we may be. For Kundera, the weight of living is found in all types of restriction, in the dense network of public and private restrictions that ultimately envelops every life in ever-tighter bonds. His novel shows us how everything in life that we choose and value for its lightness quickly reveals its own unbearable heaviness. Perhaps nothing escapes this fate but the liveliness and nimbleness of the mind—the very qualities with which the novel is written, qualities that belong to a universe other than the one we live in.

When the human realm seems doomed to heaviness, I feel the need to fly like Perseus into some other space. I am not talking about escaping into dreams or into the irrational. I mean that I feel the need to change my approach, to look at the world from a different angle, with different logic, different methods of knowing and proving. The images of lightness I'm looking for shouldn't let themselves dissolve as dreams do in the reality of the present and future . . .

In the infinite universe of literature there are always other avenues to explore, some brand-new and some exceedingly ancient, styles and forms that can change our image of the world. And when literature fails to assure me that I'm not merely chasing dreams, I look to science to sustain my visions in which all heaviness dissolves . . .

Today every branch of science seems intent on demonstrating that the world rests upon the most minute of entities: DNA messages, the pulses of neurons, quarks and neutrinos that have wandered through space since the beginning of time . . .

And then there are computers. It's true that software cannot exert the power of its lightness except through the heaviness of hardware, but it's the software that's in charge, acting on the outside world and on machines that exist solely as functions of their software and that evolve in order to run ever-more-complex programs. The second industrial revolution doesn't present us, as the first did, with overwhelming images of rolling mills or molten steel, but rather with *bits* of information that flow, as electrical impulses, through circuits. We still have machines made of steel, but they now obey bits that are weightless.

Is it legitimate to extrapolate from the discourse of science an image of the world that corresponds to my desires? If what I'm undertaking here appeals to me, it's because I feel it may be tied to a very old thread in the history of poetry.

Lucretius's *De rerum natura* is the first great poetic work in which knowledge of the world leads to a dissolution of the world's solidity and to a perception of that which is infinitely small and nimble and light. Lucretius wants to write the poem of matter, but he warns us from the start that the reality of matter is that it's made of invisible particles. He is the poet of physical concreteness, seen in its permanent, unchanging substance, but he begins by telling us that empty space is just as concrete as solid bodies. His greatest concern seems to be preventing the weight of matter from crushing us. As soon as he lays out the rigorous mechanical laws that govern every event, he feels the need to allow atoms to deviate unpredictably from the straight line, thereby ensuring the freedom both of matter and of human beings. The poetry of the invisible, the poetry of infinite unpredictable potentialities, even the poetry of nothingness, originate in this poet who has no doubts about the physical reality of the world.

This atomization of reality also extends to its visible aspects, and it's there that Lucretius shines as a poet: the dust particles that churn in a shaft of sunlight in a dark room (II, 114–124); the tiny shells, all similar yet each distinct, that a wave pushes gently onto the *bibula harena*, the thirsty sand (II, 374–376); or the spiderwebs that wind around us without our noticing them as we walk along (III, 381–390).

I have already mentioned Ovid's *Metamorphoses*, another encyclopedic poem (written half a century after Lucretius's), one rooted however not in physical reality but in the fables of mythology. For Ovid too everything can be transformed into new forms; for Ovid too knowledge of the world entails dissolving the solidity of the world; for Ovid too there is among everything that exists an essential equality that runs counter to all hierarchies of power and value. If Lucretius's world is composed of unalterable atoms, Ovid's is composed of the qualities, attributes, and forms that reveal the distinctiveness of every object and plant and animal and person but that are merely thin sheaths over a common substance which — when stirred by profound emotion — can change itself into radically different forms.

It is in tracking the change from one form to another that Ovid displays his incomparable gifts, as when he describes a woman as she realizes she is changing into a lotus tree: her feet become rooted to the ground, soft bark slowly rises to cover her groin, and she tries to tear at her hair but finds her hands full of leaves. Or when he describes Arachne's fingers, their deftness in gathering and unraveling wool, in turning a spindle, in working her embroidery needle, before suddenly showing them stretching into thin spider legs and beginning to weave webs.

For both Lucretius and Ovid, lightness is a way of seeing the world based on philosophy and science — on the doctrines of Epicurus for Lucretius, on the doctrines of Pythagoras for Ovid (a Pythagoras who, as Ovid depicts him, closely resembles Buddha). In both cases, however, this lightness is something created in the writing, using the linguistic tools of the poet, independent of whatever philosophical doctrine the poet claims to be following.

· · ·

I think my idea of lightness is starting to come into sharper focus; more than anything, I hope that what I have said so far shows that there is a lightness that is thoughtful and that is different from the frivolous lightness we all know. Indeed, thoughtful lightness can make frivolity seem heavy and opaque.

I can best illustrate this idea with a tale from the *Decameron* (VI, 9) in which the Florentine poet Guido Cavalcanti appears. Boccaccio depicts Cavalcanti as an austere philosopher walking pensively among the marble tombs beside a church. The *jeunesse dorée* of Florence were riding through the city in groups from one party to the next, looking for any opportunity to widen their circle of social invitations. Cavalcanti, despite his wealth and elegance, was not popular among them, because he never joined their reveling and because his mysterious philosophy was suspected of impiety:

> *Ora avvenne un giorno che, essendo Guido partito*
> *d'Orto San Michele e venutosene per lo Corso degli Adi-*
> *mari infino a San Giovanni, il quale spesse volte era*
> *suo cammino, essendo arche grandi di marmo, che oggi*
> *sono in Santa Reparata, e molte altre dintorno a San*
> *Giovanni, e egli essendo tralle colonne del porfido che vi*
> *sono e quelle arche e la porta di San Giovanni, che ser-*
> *rata era, messer Betto con sua brigata a caval venendo*
> *su per la piazza di Santa Reparata, vedendo Guido là*
> *tra quelle sepolture, dissero: "Andiamo a dargli briga";*
> *e spronati i cavalli, a guisa d'uno assalto sollazzevole*

gli furono, quasi prima che egli se ne avvedesse, sopra e cominciarongli a dire: "Guido, tu rifiuti d'esser di nostra brigata; ma ecco, quando tu avrai trovato che Idio non sia, che avrai fatto?"

A' quali Guido, da lor veggendosi chiuso, prestamente disse: "Signori, voi mi potete dire a casa vostra ciò che vi piace"; e posta la mano sopra una di quelle arche, che grandi erano, sì come colui che leggerissimo era, prese un salto e fusi gittato dall'altra parte, e sviluppatosi da loro se n'andò.

Then one day, having left Orto San Michele, Guido made his way down Corso degli Adimari until he reached San Giovanni, a route he often took to see the many tombs that were there, including the great marble tombs that today are in Santa Reparata, and as he walked among the porphyry columns of that place and those tombs and the door of San Giovanni, which was locked, Messer Betto and his friends came up on horseback through Piazza Santa Reparata, and seeing Guido there among the sepulchers they said, "Let's start a quarrel with him." Spurring their horses in mock attack, they were on him almost before he knew it, and they began by saying, "Guido, you refuse to join our group, but really, when you have proved that God does not exist, what will you have accomplished?" To which Guido, seeing himself surrounded, quickly replied, "Gentlemen, in your house you may say to me whatever you like," and placing his hand upon one of those tombs, which were so large, and he being so very light, he vaulted over to the other side and slipped away from them and was gone.

What interests us here is not so much the witty reply attributed to Cavalcanti (which may be interpreted in light of the fact that the poet's supposed Epicureanism was in fact Averroism, which sees the individual soul as part of the universal intellect: the tombs are your house and not mine insofar as physical death is overcome by anyone who rises to universal contemplation via intellectual speculation). What strikes us is the visual image that Boccaccio evokes: Cavalcanti freeing himself in one leap, "he being so very light."

If I had to choose an auspicious sign for the approach of the new millennium, I would choose this: the sudden nimble leap of the poet/philosopher who lifts himself against the weight of the world, proving that its heaviness contains the secret of lightness, while what many believe to be the life force of the times—loud and aggressive, roaring and rumbling—belongs to the realm of death, like a graveyard of rusted automobiles.

I'd like you to keep that image in mind while I talk about Cavalcanti, poet of lightness. The dramatis personae in his poems are less human characters than sighs, rays of light, optical images, and above all those ethereal impulses or messages that he calls "spirits." Cavalcanti takes a theme like love-sickness that isn't at all light and dissolves it into intangible entities that shift between sensitive soul and rational soul, between heart and mind, between eyes and voice. In brief, we keep encountering things that are distinguished by three qualities: 1) they're very light, 2) they're in motion, 3) they're vectors of information. In some of his poems the message-messenger is the text itself; in his most famous poem, the exiled poet addresses the ballad he's writing: "Go, lightly and softly / straight to my beloved" (*Va tu, leggera e piana / dritt'a la donna mia*). In another it is the writing implements —quill pens and the tools for trimming them—that speak: "We are the sad, bewildered quills, / the little scissors and the mournful penknife" (*Noi siàn le triste penne isbigottite, / le cesoi-uzze e'l coltellin dolente*). In one sonnet the word *spirito* or *spiritello* occurs in every line, an obvious self-parody: Cavalcanti takes his fondness for that key word to its extreme, condensing into fourteen lines a complex, abstract story involving fourteen "spirits," each with a different function. In another sonnet, the body is torn apart by heartbreak but continues to walk around like an automaton "made of copper or stone or wood" (*fatto di rame o di pietra o di legno*). In an earlier sonnet by Guinizelli, heartbreak had transformed the poet into a brass statue—a very concrete image, whose power derives precisely from the sense of weight it conveys. In Cavalcanti, the weight of the material is dissolved by the fact that the human likeness might be made of several different, and interchangeable, substances; the metaphor does not dictate a solid object, and not even the word *stone* can weigh the line down. Here too, as in Ovid and Lucretius, we find the equality of all things, which a great Italian critic, Gianfranco Contini, called the "Cavalcantian equalization of realities" (*parificazione cavalcantiana dei reali*).

The most felicitous example of this "equalization of realities" can be found in a Cavalcanti sonnet that opens with a catalog of images of beauty, all destined to be surpassed by the beauty of his beloved:

> *Biltà di donna e di saccente core*
> *e cavalieri armati che sien genti;*
> *cantar d'augelli e ragionar d'amore;*
> *adorni legni 'n mar forte correnti;*
> *aria serena quand'apar l'albore*
> *e bianca neve scender senza venti;*
> *rivera d'acqua e prato d'ogni fiore;*
> *oro, argento, azzurro 'n ornamenti . . .*

> Beauty of woman, and a wise heart's words,
> and men-at-arms and their nobility;
> the colloquies of love, the songs of birds,
> and handsome ships on the fast-running sea;
> the calmness of the air as daybreak looms,
> and white snow falling on a windless day;
> a flowing brook, a meadow full of blooms;
> silver, and gold, and lapis in array . . .

The line *"e bianca neve scender senza venti"* (and white snow falling on a windless day) was later adapted with slight variations by Dante in the *Inferno* (XIV, 30): *"come di neve in alpe sanza vento"* (like snow on mountains on a windless day). The two lines, though nearly identical, express completely different ways of thinking. In both, the snow in the absence of wind suggests a gentle, silent motion. But here the similarities end and the differences begin. In Dante the line is dominated by the specification of place (*"in alpe"*), which sets a mountain scene. In Cavalcanti, on the other hand, the adjective *bianca* ("white"), which might seem pleonastic, and the verb *scender* ("falling"), also completely predictable, together dissolve the landscape in an air of suspended abstraction. But it is above all the first word that marks the difference between the two lines. In Cavalcanti the conjunction *e* ("and") puts the snow on the same level as the other visions that come before and after it: a cascade of images, like a sample book of the world's beauties. In Dante the word *come* ("like") encloses the entire scene within the framework of metaphor, but within that framework it has its own concrete reality, just as the landscape of Hell beneath a rain of fire (which is illustrated by means of that comparison to snow) possesses a no less concrete and dramatic reality. In Cavalcanti everything moves so swiftly that we're not aware of its substance but only of its effects; in Dante everything takes on substance and stability: the weight of things is established with exactitude. Even when speaking of light things, Dante seems to want to measure the exact weight of their lightness: "like snow on mountains on a windless day." In another, very similar line, the weight of something sinking in the water and disappearing seems held back or slowed down: "like some heavy thing in dark water" (*come per acqua cupa cosa grave; Paradiso* III, 123).

At this point we must remind ourselves that the idea that the world is made up of weightless atoms surprises us because we have experienced the weight of things. Similarly, we could not admire the lightness of language if we had not also learned to admire language endowed with weight.

It might be said that two opposing literary tendencies have competed over the centuries: one that seeks to make language a weightless element that hovers over things like a cloud, or, better, a fine dust, or, better still, a magnetic field; another that seeks to imbue language with the weight and thickness and concreteness of objects and bodies and sensations.

These two paths are blazed at the beginning of Italian — and European — literature by Cavalcanti and Dante. This opposition holds true in general terms, though of course countless exceptions would have to be made, given Dante's vast wealth of resources and his extraordinary versatility. It's no coincidence that the Dante sonnet most felicitously suffused with lightness (*"Guido, i' vorrei che tu e Lapo ed io"*; "Guido, I wish that you, Lapo, and I") is dedicated to Cavalcanti. In his *Vita Nuova*, Dante treats the same subject matter as his mentor and friend, and the two poets share many words, motifs, and ideas. And when Dante wants to express lightness, even in the *Divine Comedy*, no one can do it better. But his genius lies in the opposite direction, in his ability to extract from language every sonic and emotional and sensory possibility, to capture in verse the world in all its many levels and forms and attributes, to convey the sense that the world is organized into a system, a rank, a hierarchy in which everything finds its place. To push this comparison further, I might say that Dante endows even the most abstract intellectual notion with physical heft, while Cavalcanti dissolves concrete, tangible experience in the clearly articulated rhythms of his lines, as though his thought were leaping out of the dark in rapid electrical bursts.

My brief discussion of Cavalcanti has helped clarify — at least for myself — what I mean by *lightness*. Lightness for me is related to precision and definition, not to the hazy and haphazard. Paul Valéry said, "One must be light like the bird, not like the feather" (*Il faut être léger comme l'oiseau, et non comme la plume*).

I have used Cavalcanti to illustrate at least three different kinds of lightness: Firstly, a lightening of language by which meanings are carried by a verbal fabric that seems weightless, until they take on that same rarefied consistency. I leave you to find other examples of this nature. Emily Dickinson, for one, can provide us with as many as we like:

> A sepal — petal — and a thorn
> Opon a common summer's morn —

> A flask of Dew — a Bee or two —
> A Breeze — a'caper in the trees —
> And I'm a Rose!

Secondly, the narration of a train of thought or a psychological process that involves subtle, barely perceptible elements, or any description involving a high degree of abstraction.

And here, for a more modern example, let us turn to Henry James, opening one of his books at random:

> These depths, constantly bridged over by a structure firm enough in spite of its lightness and of its occasional oscillation in the somewhat vertiginous air, invited on occasion, in the interest of their nerves, a dropping of the plummet and a measurement of the abyss. A difference had been made moreover, once for all, by the fact that she had all the while not appeared to feel the need of rebutting his charge of an idea within her that she didn't dare to express — a charge uttered just before one of the fullest of their later discussions ended.
>
> (*The Beast in the Jungle*, 1903)

Thirdly, a visual image of lightness that takes on symbolic value, as when Cavalcanti, in the Boccaccio tale, vaults nimbly over a headstone. Certain literary inventions are memorable more for what their words evoke than for the words themselves. The scene where Don Quixote runs his lance through the sail of a windmill and gets lifted into the air takes up only a few lines in the novel—it's fair to say that Cervantes invested only a fraction of his resources in the writing of it—yet it remains one of the most famous literary passages of all time.

With these guideposts I think I can begin browsing the books of my library in search of examples of lightness. In Shakespeare I turn straight to the passage in which Mercutio makes his appearance: "You are a lover; borrow Cupid's wings / and soar with them above a common bound." He is contradicting Romeo, who then replies: "Under love's heavy burden do I sink." Mercutio's way of moving through the world is defined by the first verbs he uses: *to dance, to soar, to prick*. The human visage is a mask, a "visor." Mercutio has just come onstage and already he feels the need to explain his philosophy—not with a theoretical speech, but by relating a dream of Queen Mab, "the fairies' midwife," who rides in a chariot made of "an empty hazelnut":

> Her wagon-spokes made of long spinners' legs;
> The cover, of the wings of grasshoppers;
> The traces, of the smallest spider's web;
> The collars, of the moonshine's wat'ry beams;
> Her whip, of cricket's bone; the lash, of film . . .

Let's not forget that this chariot is "drawn with a team of little atomies"—a crucial detail, I think, that allows the dream of Queen Mab to meld Lucretian atomism with Renaissance Neo-Platonism and Celtic lore.

We might also like Mercutio's dancing gait to accompany us across the threshold of the new millennium. The period that serves as backdrop to *Romeo and Juliet* has much in common with our own time: cities are bloodied by violent feuds no less senseless than those between the Montagues and Capulets; sexual liberation, as preached by the Nurse, fails to become the model of universal love; experiments are carried out with the generous optimism of Friar Laurence and his "natural philosophy," but it's never clear whether in the end they will be used for life or for death.

The Renaissance of Shakespeare's day recognized otherworldly forces connecting macrocosm and microcosm, from the Neo-Platonic heavens to the spirits of the metals that were transformed in the alchemists' crucibles. Classical mythology can offer its catalog of nymphs and dryads, but Celtic myths, with their elves and fairies, are certainly richer in imagery of the subtlest natural forces. This cultural backdrop— I'm thinking of course of Frances Yates's fascinating studies of Renaissance occult philosophy and its echoes in literature —explains why the richest illustrations of my theme are to be found in Shakespeare. I think not only of Puck and the entire phantasmagoria of *A Midsummer Night's Dream,* or of Ariel and all those who "are such stuff / As dreams are made on," but above all of the particular lyrical and existential shift that allows one's own drama to be contemplated, as if from without, and dissolved in melancholy and irony.

The weightless heaviness I mentioned in reference to Cavalcanti resurfaces in the age of Cervantes and Shakespeare: it's that particular connection between melancholy and humor that Klibansky, Panofsky, and Saxl examined in *Saturn and Melancholy* (1964). Just as melancholy is sadness made light, so humor is comedy that has lost its physical weight (that dimension of human carnality that, however, makes Boccaccio and Rabelais great) and casts doubts on the self, the world, and the entire network of relations they form.

This inextricable blend of melancholy and humor characterizes the voice of the Prince of Denmark, whose accent we have learned to recognize in all or nearly all of Shakespeare's plays, on the lips of Hamlet's many avatars. One of these, Jaques in *As You Like It* (IV, i), defines melancholy this way: "It is a melancholy of my own, compounded of many simples, extracted from many objects, and indeed the sundry contemplation of my travels, which, by often rumination, wraps me in a most humorous sadness." It is not, then, a dense or opaque melancholy, but rather a veil of minuscule particles of humors and sensations, a dusting of atoms, like everything that constitutes the basic substance of the multiplicity of things.

I confess that I am strongly tempted to depict Shakespeare as a disciple of Lucretian atomism, but I realize that would be willful. It isn't until a few decades after Shakespeare that we find, in France, the first modern writer who explicitly professes an atomistic conception of the universe in his imaginative transformation of it: Cyrano de Bergerac.

An extraordinary writer, Cyrano deserves to be better remembered, and not just as the first true precursor of science fiction but for his intellectual and poetic virtues. A follower of Gassendi's sensism and of Copernican astronomy, but influenced above all by the "natural philosophy" of the Italian Renaissance — Cardano, Bruno, Campanella — Cyrano is modern literature's first poet of atomism. In pages whose irony can't conceal a genuine cosmic excitement, Cyrano celebrates the unity of all things, animate and inanimate, the combinatorics of elementary parts that determine the diversity of life forms, and above all he conveys a sense of the precariousness of the processes that created them — that is, of how close man came to not being man, life to not being life, and the world to not being a world:

> *Vous vous étonnez comme cette matière, brouillée pêle-mêle, au gré du hasard, peut avoir constitué un homme, vu qu'il y avait tant de choses nécessaires à la construction de son être, mais vous ne savez pas que cent millions de fois cette matière, s'acheminant au dessein d'un homme, s'est arrêtée à former tantôt une pierre, tantôt du plomb, tantôt du corail, tantôt une fleur, tantôt une comète, pour le trop ou trop peu de cer-*

taines figures qu'il fallait ou ne fallait pas à désigner un homme? Si bien que ce n'est pas merveille qu'entre une infinie quantité de matière qui change et se remue incessamment, elle ait rencontré à faire le peu d'animaux, de végétaux, de minéraux que nous voyons; non plus que ce n'est pas merveille qu'en cent coups de dés il arrive une rafle. Aussi bien est-il impossible que de ce remuement il ne se fasse quelque chose, et cette chose sera toujours admirée d'un étourdi qui ne saura pas combien peu s'en est fallu qu'elle n'ait pas été faite.

(*Voyage dans la Lune*, 1657)

You marvel that this matter, scrambled willy-nilly by the hand of chance, could have come to form a man, seeing that so many things are needed for the construction of his being, but do you not know that on a hundred million occasions, when on the verge of producing a man, this matter stopped and formed a stone, or a piece of lead or coral, or a flower, or a comet, because of a lack or an excess of certain parts that were needed or not needed to build a man? It is no marvel, then, that amid an infinite amount of ever-changing and ever-shifting matter, the few animals, vegetables, and minerals that we see happened to be made, just as it is no marvel to get a pair royal after a hundred throws of the dice. It is indeed quite impossible that with all this motion some thing should not be made, and this thing will always amaze the dullard who cannot grasp how close it came to not being made

(*Voyage to the Moon*, 1657)

Continuing in this way, Cyrano at last proclaims the brotherhood of men and cabbages, and then goes on to imagine the protestations of a cabbage that is about to be cut:

Homme, mon cher frère, que t'ai-je fait qui mérite la mort? (. . .) Je me lève de terre, je m'épanouis, je te tends les bras, je t'offre mes enfants en graine, et pour récompense de ma courtoisie, tu me fais trancher la tête!

Man, dear brother of mine, what have I done to deserve death? (. . .) I arise from the earth, I blossom, I extend my arms, I offer you my seed-children, and in return for my kindness, you chop off my head!

If we keep in mind that this plea for true universal brotherhood was written nearly a century and a half before the French Revolution, we can see how the slowness of human consciousness to overcome its anthropocentric parochialism can be erased in an instant by poetic invention. And all this in the context of a voyage to the moon, in which Cyrano imaginatively surpasses his most illustrious predecessors, Lucian and Ariosto. Cyrano figures in my treatise on lightness above all for the way in which he senses, before Newton did, the problem of universal gravitation. Or rather, it is the challenge of escaping the pull of gravity that so stimulates his imagination as to lead him to invent a whole series of systems for ascending to the moon, each more ingenious than the last: using vials full of dew that evaporate in the sun; greasing himself with ox marrow, which the moon periodically sucks up; repeatedly throwing a magnetized ball straight up in the air from a chariot.

As for the magnetic method, it would be developed and perfected by Jonathan Swift to keep his flying island of Laputa aloft. In the moment when Laputa appears floating in midair, Swift's two obsessions—that is, the incorporeal abstraction of the rationalism he satirizes, and the physical weight of corporality—seem to cancel each other out in a magical equilibrium: "And I could see the sides of it, encompassed with several gradations of Galleries and Stairs, at certain intervals, to descend from one to the other. In the lowest Gallery, I beheld some People fishing with long Angling Rods, and others looking on." Swift is a contemporary and an adversary of Newton. Voltaire is an admirer of Newton, and he imagines a giant, Micromégas, who—in contrast to the giants of Swift—is defined not by his corporality but by his numerical dimensions, by spatial and temporal properties expressed in the rigorous, impassive language of scientific treatises. This logic and style allow Micromégas to travel through space from Sirius to Saturn to Earth. One might say that what strikes the literary imagination about Newton's theories is not the subjection of all things and people to their own inescapable weight but rather the balance of forces that allows celestial bodies to float in space.

The eighteenth-century imagination is full of figures suspended in air. It's no coincidence that in the early part of that century Antoine Galland's translation of *One Thousand and One Nights* had introduced the Western imagination to Eastern notions of the marvelous: flying carpets, flying horses, genies who come out of lamps. The pinnacle of that century's drive to overcome all limits via the imagination is Baron Münchausen's flight on a cannonball, an image that is forever linked in our minds with the illustration that is Gustave Doré's masterpiece. The adventures of Münchausen—which, like *One Thousand and One Nights,* may be the work of a single author, several authors, or none at all—continually defy the laws of gravity: the Baron is carried aloft by ducks, he lifts himself and his horse by pulling up on the tail of his periwig, he climbs down from the moon on a rope that he repeatedly cuts and reknots as he goes.

These images from popular literature, as well as those we've seen in more highbrow texts, go hand in hand with the literary fortunes of Newton's theories. Giacomo Leopardi, at the age of fifteen, writes an extraordinarily erudite history of astronomy, in which, among other things, he summarizes Newton's theories. The stargazing that inspired Leopardi's loveliest lines was not merely a lyrical motif; when he spoke of the moon, he knew exactly what he was talking about.

In his endless meditation on the unbearable weight of living, Leopardi associates unattainable happiness with images of lightness: birds, a female voice singing from a window, the transparency of air, and above all the moon.

From its first appearance in poetry, the moon has always had the power to communicate a sense of lightness, of suspension, of silent and calm enchantment. Early on, I had planned to devote this entire talk to the moon, tracing its appearances in the literatures of various times and places. But then I decided to leave the moon entirely to Leopardi. Because Leopardi's miracle was to subtract so much weight from language that it came to resemble moonlight. The many appearances of the moon in his verse take up only a handful of lines, but they suffice to bathe whole poems in its light or to cast upon them the shadow of its absence.

> *Dolce e chiara è la notte e senza vento,*
> *e queta sovra i tetti e in mezzo agli orti*
> *posa la luna, e di lontan rivela*
> *serena ogni montagna.*
> . . .
> *O graziosa luna, io mi rammento*
> *che, or volge l'anno, sovra questo colle*
> *io venia pien d'angoscia a rimirarti:*
> *e tu pendevi allor su quella selva*

siccome or fai, che tutta la rischiari.

. . .

O cara luna, al cui tranquillo raggio
danzan le lepri nelle selve . . .

. . .

Già tutta l'aria imbruna,
torna azzurro il sereno, e tornan l'ombre
giù da' colli e da' tetti
al biancheggiar della recente luna.

. . .

Che fai tu, luna, in ciel? dimmi, che fai,
silenziosa luna?
Sorgi la sera, e vai,
contemplando i deserti; indi ti posi.

The night is mild and clear and without wind,
And in the gardens and above the roofs
The moon in silence rests, and in the distance
Reveals each peaceful mountain.

. . .

O graceful moon, now that a year has passed,
I call once more to mind how, filled with anguish,
I climbed this hill to gaze on you again:
And you were hanging there, above that forest,
As you are now, brightening everything.

. . .

O cherished moon, beneath whose peaceful rays
Hares in the forests dance . . .

. . .
Now all the air grows dim,
The bright sky turns dark blue, and shadows come
Down from the hills and roofs
Beneath the whitening of the recent moon.
. . .
What are you doing, moon, there in the sky?
Tell me, silent moon, what?
You rise in the evening, and pass by,
Pondering wastelands. Then you set.

I've woven a lot of threads into this talk, haven't I? Which should I tug to lay my hands on the conclusion? There's the thread that connects the moon, Leopardi, Newton, gravitation and levitation . . . The thread of Lucretius, atomism, Cavalcanti's philosophy of love, Renaissance magic, Cyrano . . . Then there's the thread about writing as metaphor for the particulate substance of the world: already for Lucretius letters were atoms in constant motion, whose permutations created the most various words and sounds—an idea later taken up by a long line of thinkers for whom the secrets of the world were contained in the combinatorics of written signs. Consider the *Ars Magna* of Ramon Llull, or the kabbalah of the Spanish rabbis or of Pico della Mirandola . . . Galileo too saw the alphabet as the model for every combinatorics of minimal units . . . And then there's Leibniz . . .

Must I go down that road? Won't the conclusion that awaits me sound too pat? Writing: the model of every process of reality . . . indeed, the only knowable reality . . . indeed, the only reality at all . . . No, I won't go down that one-way road, which takes me too far from my understanding of how words are used, which is as a perpetual pursuit of things, a way of adapting to their infinite variety.

One thread still remains, one I began to unspool at the beginning of this talk: literature as an existential function, the search for lightness as a reaction to the weight of living. Perhaps even Lucretius and Ovid felt this need: Lucretius, who sought—or believed he was seeking—Epicurean ataraxia, and Ovid, who sought—or believed he was seeking—Pythagorean reincarnation into other lives.

I'm accustomed to thinking of literature as a search for knowledge; in order to move onto existential terrain I need to consider it in relation to anthropology, ethnology, and mythology.

In response to the precariousness of tribal existence—drought, sickness, evil forces—a shaman would nullify the weight of his body and fly to another world, another level of perception, where he might find the strength to alter reality. In centuries and civilizations closer to our own, in villages where women bore most of the weight of a restricted life, witches flew by night on broomsticks and on even lighter contraptions, such as wheat-ears or pieces of straw. Before being codified by the Inquisition, these visions formed part of the popular imagination, and we might even say of actual experience. I consider it an anthropological constant, this nexus between the levitation desired and the deprivation suffered. It's this anthropological mechanism that literature perpetuates—especially oral literature. In folktales the flight to another world is a common occurrence. It is one of the "functions" catalogued by Vladimir Propp in his *Morfologija skazki* (*Morphology of the Folktale*, 1928), one of the methods of "transference of the hero." It is defined as follows: "Usually the object of the search is found in 'another' or 'different' realm, which may be located very far away horizontally or at a great vertical height or depth." Propp goes on to list various instances in which "the hero flies through the air": on the back of a horse or bird, taking the form of a bird, on a flying ship, on a flying carpet, on the back of a giant or spirit, in the carriage of the devil, and so on.

I don't think it's a stretch to connect the function of shamans and witches documented by ethnologists and folklorists to the literary imagination; on the contrary, I think that the most profound rationale for any literary act may be sought in the anthropological necessities to which it responds.

I would like to close my talk by calling to mind a Kafka story, "Der Kübelreiter" ("The Bucket Rider"). A brief first-person story written in 1917, it originated in what was clearly a very real predicament during that wartime winter, the worst of the Austrian Empire: a coal shortage. The narrator leaves home with an empty bucket in search of coal for his stove. On the road the bucket serves him as a horse; indeed, it lifts him as high as the second story of a house and carries him, rocking, as if on a camel's back.

The coal dealer's shop is underground and the bucket rider is too high up; he struggles to make himself heard by the man, who seems willing to help, while the man's wife refuses to hear him. The rider begs them to give him a shovelful of their poorest coal, even though he can't pay at the moment. The coal dealer's wife unties her apron and shoos away the intruder as if he were a fly. The bucket is so light that it soars off with its rider and disappears beyond the Ice Mountains.

Kafka's stories are often mysterious, and this one more so than most. Perhaps Kafka simply wanted to tell us how going out in search of a bit of coal, on a cold night in wartime, can —with the simple swing of an empty bucket—turn into the quest of a knight-errant, a caravan crossing a desert, a magical flight. But this idea of an empty bucket that can lift you beyond the aid and also the greed of others, an empty bucket that stands for deprivation and desire and pursuit, that lifts you so high that your humble plea can no longer be granted —this idea opens the way to endless reflection.

I have spoken of shamans and of folk heroes, of deprivation that transforms into lightness, making it possible to fly to a realm where every shortage will be magically replenished. I've spoken of witches who fly on humble household implements not unlike buckets. But the hero of this story by Kafka doesn't seem endowed with the powers of the shaman or the witch, nor does the realm beyond the Ice Mountains seem one in which the empty bucket might find something to refill it. Besides, as soon as it was full it would be unable to fly. That is how we, astride our bucket, will face the new millennium: without hoping to find there anything more than we're able to bring with us. Lightness, for example, whose virtues this talk has tried to illustrate.

2

Quickness

I'll start by telling you an old legend.

Late in life the emperor Charlemagne fell in love with a German girl. The court barons were dismayed to see that their sovereign, overcome by ardent desire and forgetful of royal dignity, was neglecting imperial affairs. When the girl suddenly died, the dignitaries sighed with relief — but only briefly, for Charlemagne's love did not die with the girl. The emperor had the embalmed body brought to his chamber and refused to leave its side. Archbishop Turpin, alarmed by this morbid passion and suspecting some enchantment, decided to examine the corpse. Hidden beneath the dead tongue he found a gemstone ring. As soon as he took possession of it, Charlemagne hastened to have the corpse buried and directed his love toward the person of the archbishop. To extricate himself from that awkward situation, Turpin threw the ring into Lake Constance. Charlemagne fell in love with the lake and refused to leave its shores.

This legend, "taken from a book on magic," is recounted even more tersely than I have done here in an unpublished notebook by the French Romantic writer Barbey d'Aurevilly. (It can be found in the Pléiade edition of his works: vol. 1, p. 1315.) Ever since I read it, my mind has kept returning to it, as if the ring's enchantment were still exerting its pull through the story.

Let's try to figure out why a story like this one fascinates us. We have a series of events, all of them unusual, that form a chain—an old man's infatuation with a young girl, a necrophiliac obsession, a homosexual attraction—at the end of which everything subsides into melancholy contemplation: the old king gazing raptly at the lake. "Charlemagne, his gaze fixed on his Lake Constance, in love with the hidden abyss" (*Charlemagne, la vue attachée sur son lac de Constance, amoureux de l'abîme caché*), writes Barbey d'Aurevilly in the passage of the novel (*Une vieille maîtresse*, p. 221) whose footnote refers us to the legend.

This chain of events is linked by a verbal element, the word *love* or *passion*, which establishes a continuity among different kinds of attraction, and by a narrative element, the magic ring, which establishes a logical relation of cause and effect among the various episodes. The rush of desire toward an object that doesn't exist, an absence, a lack—symbolized by the empty circle of the ring—is created more by the rhythm of the story than by the events narrated. In the same way, the whole story is shot through with a feeling of death, against which Charlemagne desperately struggles, clinging to what links him to life until his desperation subsides in contemplation of the lake.

The story's true protagonist, however, is the magic ring, for it is the movement of the ring that dictates the movements of the characters and defines the relationships among them. Around the magic object there forms a kind of force field, which is the field of the story. We might say that the magic object is an outward sign that makes visible the links among characters and among events—a narrative function that goes back to Norse sagas and chivalric romances and that continues to surface in Italian Renaissance epics. In *Orlando Furioso* we witness an endless series of exchanges of swords, shields, helmets, and horses, each endowed with particular properties, such that the plot can be described through changes in the properties of certain objects endowed with certain powers, which define the relations among certain characters.

In realistic fiction, Mambrino's helmet can become a barber's basin, but it doesn't lose importance or meaning. Similarly, every object that Robinson Crusoe salvages from the wrecked ship or fashions with his own hands takes on crucial importance. We might say that as soon as an object appears in a narrative, it becomes charged with special force, becomes like the pole in a magnetic field or a node in an invisible network of relations. The object's symbolic value can be explicit or not, but it is always present. We might even say that any object in a narrative is a magic object.

But back to the legend of Charlemagne, which in Italian literature has a tradition behind it. In his *Lettere familiari* (I.4), Petrarch describes how he heard this "pleasing little tale" (*fabella non inamena*), which he says he didn't believe, while visiting Charlemagne's tomb in Aachen. In Petrarch's Latin, the story is much richer both in sensory detail—the bishop of Cologne, heeding a miraculous divine instruction, sticks a finger beneath the corpse's cold, stiff tongue (*"sub gelida rigentique lingua"*)—and in moral commentary. But I find the bare-bones version, in which everything is left to the imagination and the quickness of events creates a sense of inevitability, much more powerful.

Several versions of the legend appear, with greater emphasis on the necrophiliac element, in the flowery Italian of the sixteenth century. Sebastiano Erizzo, a Venetian short story writer, has Charlemagne utter, while in bed with the corpse, a lamentation of several pages. On the other hand, his homosexual passion for the bishop is barely mentioned or even omitted, as in Giuseppe Betussi's famous sixteenth-century treatise on love, where the story ends with the discovery of the ring. And speaking of the ending: in Petrarch and his Italian followers, Lake Constance doesn't appear; the action is set entirely in Aachen, since the legend is meant to explain the origins of the palace and temple built there by the emperor. The ring gets tossed into a swamp, and he inhales the muddy stench like a perfume and "delights in taking the waters" (*usa le acque con grande voluttà*)—details that recall other local legends about the origins of thermal springs and that further emphasize the deathly mood of the whole.

Earlier still were the medieval German traditions studied by Gaston Paris, in which Charlemagne's love for the dead woman is varied in ways that make it a very different story:

sometimes the beloved is the emperor's lawful wife, who uses the magic ring to ensure his fidelity; sometimes she is a fairy or nymph who dies as soon as the ring is taken from her; sometimes she is a woman who seems alive but is revealed, once the ring is taken, to be a corpse. A Scandinavian saga is the likely source: the Norse king Harald sleeps with his dead wife, who is wrapped in a magic mantle that makes her seem alive. In short, the medieval versions collected by Gaston Paris lack the chainlike succession of events, and the literary versions by Petrarch and the Renaissance writers lack quickness. That's why I continue to prefer the version reported by Barbey d'Aurevilly, despite its coarse, patchwork quality. Its secret lies in its economy: events, regardless of their duration, become like points connected by straight-line segments in a zigzag fashion that suggests unceasing motion.

I don't mean to say here that quickness has value in itself. Narrative time can also be delaying, cyclic, or static. In any case, a story is an operation on duration, an enchantment that affects the flow of time, contracting it or expanding it. Sicilian storytellers use the expression "stories take no time" (*lu cuntu nun metti tempo*) when they want to skip over things or indicate the passage of months or years. The craft of oral storytelling in the popular tradition is shaped by functional concerns; it omits pointless details and insists on repetition, as when, for example, a fable consists of obstacles that must be overcome. Part of a child's pleasure in listening to stories is in the anticipation of certain kinds of repetition: situations, expressions, stock phrases. Just as rhymes help mark the rhythm of poems and songs, events can rhyme in prose narratives. That narrative of the Charlemagne legend works because there is a series of events that correspond like rhymes in a poem.

If during a certain period of my writing life I was drawn to folktales and fairy tales, it wasn't out of loyalty to some ethnic tradition (my roots are in a wholly modern, cosmopolitan Italy), nor out of nostalgia for the stories of my childhood (in my family, children read only educational, science-based books), but rather out of my interest in their style and structure, in the economy, rhythm, and basic logic that govern their telling. As I worked to transcribe the Italian folktales taken down by nineteenth-century scholars of folklore, I took special pleasure when the original texts were quite brief and I, retelling them in my *Fiabe italiane* (*Italian Folktales*, 1956), had to preserve their concision while trying to maximize their narrative power and poetic appeal. For example, tale 57 begins like this:

> *Un Re s'ammalò. Vennero i medici e gli dissero: "Senta, Maestà, se vuol guarire, bisogna che lei prenda una penna dell'Orco. È un rimedio difficile, perché l'Orco tutti i cristiani che vede se li mangia".*
>
> *Il Re lo disse a tutti ma nessuno ci voleva andare. Lo chiese a un suo sottoposto, molto fedele e coraggioso, e questi disse: "Andrò".*

*Gli insegnarono la strada: "In cima a un monte, ci
sono sette buche: in una delle sette, ci sta l'Orco".*

*L'uomo andò e lo prese il buio per la strada. Si fermò
in una locanda . . .*

A King fell ill. The doctors came and said, "Listen,
Majesty, if you want to get well, you have to get a
feather from the Ogre. That will be hard, since the
Ogre eats every soul he sees."

The King spread the word, but no one wanted
to go. He asked a retainer who was very loyal and
brave, and this man said, "I will go."

They showed him the way: "On top of a mountain are seven caves; in one of the seven, the Ogre
lives."

The man set out and darkness overtook him
along the way. He stopped at an inn . . .

Nothing is said about what illness the king suffered from,
or how an ogre could possibly have feathers, or what those
caves were like. But everything that is mentioned plays a necessary role in the plot. The chief characteristic of the folktale
is economy of expression; the most extraordinary adventures
are recounted in terms of their bare essentials. There is always a battle against time, against obstacles that impede or
delay the achievement of a desire or the recovery of a lost
possession. Time can be stopped completely, as in Sleeping
Beauty's castle; all Charles Perrault has to do is to write:

les broches mêmes qui étaient au feu toutes pleines de perdrix et de faisans s'endormirent, et le feu aussi. Tout cela se fit en un moment: les fées n'étaient pas longues à leur besogne.

even the spits over the fire, laden with partridge and pheasant, went to sleep, and the fire slept too. It all happened in an instant; the fairies were not long in their labor.

The relativity of time is an almost universal theme of folktales: a journey to some faraway land seems to last only a few hours, yet the traveler returns to find the place he left unrecognizable, many years having passed. Here I might mention that in the early days of American literature this motif gave rise to Washington Irving's "Rip Van Winkle," which acquired the status of a foundation myth for your change-based society.

This motif can also be understood as an allegory of narrative time, of its lack of correspondence to real time. And the same significance can be recognized in the opposite operation, characteristic of Oriental storytelling, in which time expands by means of an internal proliferation from one story to another. Scheherazade tells a story in which someone tells a story in which someone tells a story, and so on.

The art that allows Scheherazade to save her own life each night consists in knowing how to link one story to the other and also how to break off at just the right time — two operations on the continuity and discontinuity of time. It is a secret of rhythm, of mastering time, that we can trace to its origins: to the effects of meter in epic verse, and to the effects in prose narrative that make us want to hear what happens next.

Everyone knows how awkward it feels to hear someone who can't tell jokes try to tell one, only to spoil the effects, by which I mean above all the linkages and the rhythms. This feeling is evoked in one of Boccaccio's tales (VI, 1), which is dedicated precisely to the art of oral storytelling.

After dining as the guests of a Florentine lady at her country house, a cheerful group of knights and ladies set out on foot for another pleasant place in the area. To ease their journey, one of the men offers to tell a story:

> "*Madonna Oretta, quando voi vogliate, io vi porterò, gran parte della via che a andare abbiamo, a cavallo con una delle belle novelle del mondo*".
>
> *Al quale la donna rispuose: "Messere, anzi ve ne priego io molto, e sarammi carissimo".*
>
> *Messer lo cavaliere, al quale forse non stava meglio la spada allato che 'l novellar nella lingua, udito questo, cominciò una sua novella, la quale nel vero da sé era bellissima, ma egli or tre e quattro e sei volte replicando una medesima parola e ora indietro tornando e talvolta dicendo: "Io non dissi bene" e spesso ne' nomi errando, un per un altro ponendone, fieramente la guastava: senza che egli pessimamente, secondo le qualità delle persone e gli atti che accadevano, profereva.*

*Di che a madonna Oretta, udendolo, spesse volte
veniva un sudore e uno sfinimento di cuore, come se in-
ferma fosse stata per terminare; la qual cosa poi che più
sofferir non poté, conoscendo che il cavaliere era entrato
nel pecoreccio né era per riuscirne, piacevolmente disse:
"Messer, questo vostro cavallo ha troppo duro trotto, per
che io vi priego che vi piaccia di pormi a piè.*

"Lady Oretta, if you wish, I could give you a ride
for much of our remaining journey—a ride on
the back of one of the finest tales in the world."

To which the lady replied: "Sir, I beg you to do
so; it would be a joy to me."

Hearing this, the knight, who likely wore a
sword at his side no better than a tale on his
tongue, began to tell a story—which of itself was
in fact quite fine, but by repeating the same word
three or four or six times, or by backing up and
sometimes saying, "I didn't say that well," or by
frequently getting names wrong, substituting one
for another, he ruined it mercilessly. Aside from
which, his delivery, given the nature of his characters and the events that were transpiring, was
terrible.

As a result, Lady Oretta, as she listened, often
found herself in a sweat, her heart faltering, as if
she were sick and nearing her end. Finally, unable
to suffer the thing any longer, and seeing that the

knight had gotten himself into a mess and was unlikely to get himself out of it, said pleasantly, "Sir,
this horse of yours has too hard a trot, so I beg you
to kindly set me back on my feet."

The story is a horse, a means of transport, with a particular
gait—trot or gallop—depending on the route to be traveled.
And the speed at issue is a mental speed. The clumsy narrator's shortcomings, as enumerated by Boccaccio, are above
all offenses against rhythm, but they are also defects of style,
because the story's expressions are poorly suited to its characters and actions. It is clear, then, that even proper style requires a readiness to adapt, a nimbleness of expression and
thought.

The horse as emblem of mental speed has marked the
whole history of literature, prefiguring all the problems particular to our own technological situation. The era of speed,
in transportation as in information, begins with one of the
finest essays in English literature, "The English Mail-Coach,"
by Thomas De Quincey, who in 1849 already understood
everything we know today about the world of motors and
highways, including fatal high-speed crashes.

De Quincey describes a nighttime trip seated on the box of
an extremely fast mail coach alongside a gigantic coachman
who is fast asleep. The technical perfection of the vehicle
together with the driver's transformation into a blind inanimate object puts the traveler at the mercy of the inexorable
exactitude of a machine. His senses heightened by a dose of

laudanum, De Quincey realizes that the horses are running at a speed of thirteen miles per hour on the *wrong* side of the road. This means certain disaster—not for the very fast and very bulky mail coach but rather for the first unlucky carriage that happens along the same road in the opposite direction. Indeed, at the end of a straight, tree-lined avenue that resembles a cathedral nave, he sees a young couple approaching in a "frail reedy gig" at one mile per hour: "Between them and eternity, to all human calculation, there is but a minute and a half." De Quincey shouts. "Mine had been the first step; the second was for the young man; the third was for God." The account of these few seconds remains unsurpassed, even in a period when the experience of high speeds has become a basic fact of human life.

> Glance of eye, thought of man, wing of angel, which of these had speed enough to sweep between the question and the answer, and divide the one from the other? Light does not tread upon the steps of light more indivisibly than did our all-conquering arrival upon the escaping efforts of the gig.

De Quincey manages to convey the sense of an extremely brief span of time that nonetheless contains both the calculation of the technical inevitability of the crash and also the incalculable—God's part—thanks to which the two vehicles do not collide.

What is of interest to us here is not physical speed but the relation between physical and mental speed. That relation was also of interest to a great Italian poet of De Quincey's generation. Giacomo Leopardi, who had an extraordinarily sedentary youth, described in an entry in his notebooks, the *Zibaldone*, a rare moment of joy:

> *La velocità, per esempio, de' cavalli o veduta, o speri-mentata, cioè quando essi vi trasportano (. . .) è pia-cevolissima per sé sola, cioè per la vivacità, l'energia, la forza, la vita di tal sensazione. Essa desta realmente una quasi idea dell'infinito, sublima l'anima, la forti-fica . . .*
>
> (27 ottobre 1821)

> The speed, for instance, of horses, whether imag-ined or experienced, that is, when they are carry-ing you [. . .] is enormously pleasurable in itself, because of the vividness, the energy, the strength, the life of such a sensation. It truly wakens some-thing like an idea of the infinite, it exalts the mind, fortifies it . . .
>
> (October 27, 1821)

In the same notebooks, over the succeeding months, Leo-pardi developed his reflections on speed, and at a certain point he began discussing style:

La rapidità e la concisione dello stile piace perché presenta all'anima una folla d'idee simultanee, così rapidamente succedentisi, che paiono simultanee, e fanno ondeggiar l'anima in una tale abbondanza di pensieri, o d'immagini e sensazioni spirituali, ch'ella o non è capace di abbracciarle tutte, e pienamente ciascuna, o non ha tempo di restare in ozio, e priva di sensazioni. La forza dello stile poetico, che in gran parte è tutt'uno colla rapidità, non è piacevole per altro che per questi effetti, e non consiste in altro. L'eccitamento d'idee simultanee, può derivare e da ciascuna parola isolata, o propria o metaforica, e dalla loro collocazione, e dal giro della frase, e dalla soppressione stessa di altre parole o frasi ec.

(3 novembre 1821)

A quick, concise style is pleasing because it offers the mind a host of ideas simultaneously, or in such rapid succession that they appear simultaneous, staggering the mind with such an abundance of thoughts, or of psychic images and sensations, that either it is unable to encompass all of them, and any of them fully, or it has no time to remain idle, empty of sensations. The power of poetic style, which is largely the same thing as quickness, is pleasing for such effects alone, and consists of nothing else. The excitement of simultaneous ideas can derive from individual words, whether literal or metaphorical, from their arrangement, from a turn of phrase, and even from the suppression of other words and phrases, etc.

(November 3, 1821)

The metaphor of the horse for speed of mind was, to my knowledge, first used by Galileo. In *Il Saggiatore* (*The Assayer*, 1623), as he debated a rival who backed up his claims with many classical quotations, he wrote:

> *Se il discorrere circa un problema difficile fosse come il portar pesi, dove molti cavalli porteranno più sacca di grano che un caval solo, io acconsentirei che i molti discorsi facessero più che un solo; ma il discorrere è come il correre, e non come il portare, ed un caval barbero solo correrà più che cento frisoni.* (45)

If discoursing about a difficult problem were like carrying weights, where many horses can carry more sacks of grain than a single horse, I would agree that many discourses could do more than just one. But discoursing is like coursing, not like carrying, and one Barbary courser can outrun a hundred Friesians.

For Galileo, discoursing means reasoning, and often deductive reasoning. The statement "discoursing is like coursing"

(*il discorrere è come il correre*) could be his stylistic credo—
style as method of thought and as literary taste. Quickness
and nimbleness of thought, economy of argument, and also
imaginative examples—for Galileo, these are the qualities
crucial to good thinking.

Galileo also demonstrates a fondness for horses in his metaphors and *Gedankenexperimenten*. In a study I once did of his
use of metaphor, I counted at least eleven notable examples
in which he mentions horses: as an image of movement, and
thus as a tool for experiments in kinetics; as a form of nature in all its complexity and also all its beauty; as a form that
sparks the imagination in scenarios where horses undergo
the most unlikely trials or grow to enormous size—all in
addition to his identification of reasoning with racing ("discoursing is like coursing").

In *Dialogo sopra i due massimi sistemi del mondo* (*Dialogue
Concerning the Two Chief World Systems,* 1632), speed of
thought is personified by Sagredo, a character who engages
in discussions with the Ptolemaic Simplicio and the Copernican Salviati. Salviati and Sagredo represent two different facets of Galileo's personality. Salviati, the rigorous, methodical
reasoner, proceeds slowly and carefully. Sagredo, characterized by his "extremely rapid speech" and a more imaginative
spirit, has a tendency to draw unproven conclusions and to
push every idea to its extreme, as when he speculates about
what life might be like on the moon or what would happen if
the earth stopped turning.

It is Salviati, however, who defines the value system in

which Galileo locates intellectual speed. The mind of God, he argues, reasons instantaneously, not by steps, and is thus infinitely superior to the human mind, which should not, however, be discounted or considered worthless, since it was created by God, and since it has in its step-by-step fashion understood and explored and accomplished marvelous things. At this point Sagredo breaks in to praise the greatest human invention, the alphabet:

Ma sopra tutte le invenzioni stupende, qual eminenza di mente fu quella di colui che s'immaginò di trovar modo di comunicare i suoi più reconditi pensieri a qualsivoglia altra persona, benché distante per lunghissimo intervallo di luogo e di tempo? parlare con quelli che son nell'Indie, parlare a quelli che non sono ancora nati né saranno se non di qua a mille e dieci mila anni? e con qual facilità? con i vari accozzamenti di venti caratteruzzi sopra una carta.

But above all stupendous inventions, what eminence of mind was his who imagined he could find a way to communicate his inmost thoughts to any other person, even if separated by vast intervals of space and time? To speak with people in the Indies, to speak with those who are not yet born and will not be for a thousand or ten thousand years? And with such ease? All by the different arrangements of twenty little letters on a page.

In my previous talk, on lightness, I quoted Lucretius, who saw in the combinatorics of the alphabet a model for the intangible atomic structure of matter. Today I quote Galileo, who saw in the permutations of the alphabet — "the different arrangements of twenty little letters" (*i vari accozzamenti di venti caratteruzzi*) — an unsurpassed tool of communication. Communication among people separated by space and time, he says — but one ought to add the immediate communication that writing establishes between every existent or possible thing.

In each of these talks I'm choosing a particular quality dear to my heart to recommend to the next millennium, and today the quality I want to recommend is this: in an age dominated by other media that are much faster and more pervasive and that risk flattening all communication into a single, homogenous crust, the function of literature is to communicate among different things in terms of their differences, exalting rather than diminishing their differences, which is the proper role of written language.

The motor age has turned speed into a measurable value, with speed records marking the history of the progress of machines and men. But speed of mind cannot be measured and does not allow for comparisons or competitions, nor can its results be ranked to give historical perspective. Speed of mind is valuable in itself, for the pleasure it gives those susceptible to such pleasure, not for any practical use it can be put to. Fast thinking is not necessarily better than considered thinking—far from it. But it conveys something special that has to do specifically with its swiftness.

The qualities I have chosen as subjects for these lectures do not, as I said at the start, exclude their opposite qualities. Just as my respect for weight was implicit in my praise of lightness, so this defense of quickness does not presume to deny the pleasures of delay. Literature has developed various strategies for slowing the flow of time; I have already mentioned repetition, and now I should say a word about digression.

In real life, time is a resource we are stingy with. In literature, time is a resource to be disposed of in a casual, leisurely fashion—it's not a question of crossing some finish line first. On the other hand, being thrifty with time is a good thing, since the more time we save, the more we'll be able to lose. Quickness of style and thought means above all nimbleness, mobility, and ease—all qualities that go with writing that is prone to digression, to leaping from one topic to another, to losing the thread a hundred times and finding it again after a hundred twists and turns.

Laurence Sterne's great invention was a novel composed entirely of digressions, an example soon followed by Diderot. The divagation or digression is a way to postpone the ending, a proliferation of the internal time of a work, a perpetual attempt to escape—but to escape from what? From death, of course, according to an introduction to *Tristram Shandy* written by the Italian writer Carlo Levi, whom few would have pegged as a Sterne admirer. Levi's secret, however, was to bring precisely that digressive spirit and sense of limitless time to the examination of social problems. He writes:

L'orologio è il primo simbolo di Shandy; sotto il suo influsso egli viene generato, ed iniziano le sue disgrazie, che sono tutt'uno con questo segno del tempo. La morte sta nascosta negli orologi, come diceva il Belli; e l'infelicità della vita individuale, di questo frammento, di questa cosa scissa e disgregata, e priva di totalità: la morte, che è il tempo, il tempo della individuazione, della separazione, l'astratto tempo che rotola verso la sua fine. Tristram Shandy non vuol nascere, perché non vuol morire. Tutti i mezzi, tutte le armi sono buone per salvarsi dalla morte e dal tempo. Se la linea retta è la più breve fra due punti fatali e inevitabili, le digressioni la allungheranno: e se queste digressioni diventeranno così complesse, aggrovigliate, tortuose, così rapide da far perdere le proprie tracce, chissà che la morte non ci trovi più, che il tempo si smarrisca, e che possiamo restare celati nei mutevoli nascondigli.

The clock is Shandy's first symbol: under its influence, he is conceived and his misfortunes begin, which are the same thing according to this sign of time. Death is hidden in clocks, as Belli said, along with the unhappiness of individual life, of this fragment, of this thing that is divided, disintegrated, deprived of wholeness—death, which is time, the time of individuation, of separation, the abstract time that rolls toward its end. Tristram Shandy doesn't want to be born because he doesn't want to die. Any means, any weapon, can be used to save oneself from death and time. If a straight line is the shortest distance between two fatal, inescapable points, then digressions lengthen that line — and if these digressions become so complex, tangled, tortuous, and so rapid as to obscure their own tracks, then perhaps death won't find us again, perhaps time will lose its way, perhaps we'll be able to remain concealed in our ever-changing hiding places.

These are words that give me pause — because I am not a devotee of digression. I might say I prefer to entrust myself to the straight line, in the hopes that it will continue on into infinity and make me unreachable. I prefer to carefully calculate my escape trajectory, eager to launch myself like an arrow and disappear over the horizon. Or, if too many obstacles block my path, to calculate the series of straight segments that will get me out of the labyrinth as soon as possible.

In my youth I chose as my motto the ancient Latin maxim *festina lente* — make haste slowly. Perhaps what attracted me even more than the words or the idea were its evocative emblems. You may recall the title pages of Aldus Manutius, the great Venetian humanist and publisher, on which the motto *festina lente* was symbolized by a dolphin snaking around the shank of an anchor. That elegant printer's mark, about which Erasmus wrote some memorable pages, suggests the intensity and tenacity of intellectual labor. But both dolphin and anchor belong to the realm of marine imagery, while I have always preferred emblems that, like a rebus, combine incongruous, enigmatic figures — such as the butterfly and crab with which Paolo Giovio illustrated *festina lente* in his sixteenth-century collection of emblems: two animal shapes, both bizarre, both symmetrical, that create between themselves an unexpected harmony.

From its beginnings, my work as a writer has aimed to follow the lightning-fast course of mental circuits that capture and link points that are far apart in space and time. In my fondness for adventure stories and fairy tales, I have always sought something like an inner energy, a motion of the mind. I have focused on the image and on the motion that springs naturally from the image, knowing all the while that one cannot speak of a literary result until this stream of imagination becomes words. As for the writer of verse, so for the writer of prose: success is in the felicity of verbal expression, which can sometimes be achieved by a flash of inspiration but which normally entails a patient search for the *mot juste*, for the sentence in which no word can be replaced, for the most efficient and semantically dense arrangements of sounds and ideas. I am convinced that writing prose should be no different from writing poetry; both seek a mode of expression that is necessary, singular, dense, concise, and memorable.

It's hard to maintain this kind of tension in very long

works, and in any case my temperament leads me to feel most at home in briefer pieces; my work consists largely of what you call "short stories." For example, the kind of task I set myself in *Le cosmicomiche* (*Cosmicomics,* 1965) and *T con zero* (*t zero,* 1967)—giving narrative shape to abstract ideas of space and time—could work only within the brief span of a short story. And in *Le città invisibili* (*Invisible Cities,* 1972), and now in the descriptions of *Palomar* (*Mr. Palomar,* 1983), I've tried even shorter forms, with even less narrative development: something between parables and prose poems. Of course the length or brevity of a text is an external measure, but I'm referring to a particular density that, even if it can also be achieved in longer-form narratives, nevertheless must be measured page by page.

In this fondness for shorter forms I am merely following the true inclination of Italian literature, which is poor in novelists but always rich in poets, who even when writing in prose are at their best in texts where the heights of imagination and thought are contained in a few pages—texts such as Leopardi's *Operette morali* (Little moral works), which has no peer in other literatures.

American literature has a glorious and still thriving tradition of short stories—indeed, I would say that its crown jewels are among them. But the rigidly bipartisan taxonomy of publishers—either short stories or novels—leaves out other kinds of short forms, which nonetheless can be seen in the prose works of great American poets, from the *Specimen Days* of Walt Whitman to many pages of William Carlos Williams.

The demands of the publishing marketplace are a fetish that should not prevent experimentation with new forms. I hope here to wave a flag for the richness of short forms, with all they presuppose in terms of style and density of content. I'm thinking of Paul Valéry's *Monsieur Teste* and many of his essays, of Francis Ponge's prose poems about objects, of Michel Leiris's explorations of himself and his own language, and of the extremely brief stories in Henri Michaux's *Plume,* with their mysterious and hallucinatory humor.

The greatest new literary genre of our time was invented by a master of short forms, Jorge Luis Borges, when he invented himself as narrator—this being the "egg of Columbus" that enabled him to overcome the block which, until he was nearly forty, kept him from moving from essayistic prose to narrative prose. Borges's idea was to pretend that the book he wanted to write had already been written—written by someone else, some imaginary unknown author, working in a different language, a different culture—and then to describe, summarize, and review that imaginary book. According to an anecdote that's now part of Borges lore, when the first extraordinary story written along these lines, "El acercamiento a Almotásim" ("The Approach to Al-Mu'tasim"), appeared in the journal *Sur* in 1940, it was indeed believed to be a review of a book by an Indian author. Similarly it has become obligatory among Borges critics to observe that all his texts double or multiply their own space through other books (whether classical, scholarly, or simply invented) from real or imagined libraries. What I especially want to emphasize is the way Borges opens his windows onto the infinite without the slightest busyness, in a style that's utterly clear and sober and airy — as if telling stories through summaries and glimpses results in the most precise and concrete language, the inventiveness of which lies in its rhythmic variety, its syntactic movement, its unexpected and surprising adjectives. With Borges is born a literature raised to its square and at the same time a literature as the extraction of its own square root: a "potential literature," as it would be called later in France, but whose heralds may be found in *Ficciones,* in the cues and procedures of what might have been the words of an imaginary author called Herbert Quain.

Concision is just one aspect of the subject I have chosen to discuss, and I'll restrict myself to telling you that I dream of encompassing vast cosmologies, sagas, and epics in the scope of an epigram. In the ever-busier times that await us, literature will need to aim for the highest concentration of poetry and thought.

Borges and Bioy Casares assembled an anthology called *Cuentos breves y extraordinarios (Short and Extraordinary Tales,* 1955). I would like to put together a collection of stories consisting of a single sentence, or if possible a single line. But so far I haven't found any that surpass the one by the Guatemalan writer Augusto Monterroso: "When he awoke, the dinosaur was still there" (*Cuando despertò, el dinosaurio todavìa estaba allì*).

I realize that this lecture, based as it is on invisible connections, has branched out in various directions and risks seeming scattered. But all the topics I have discussed this evening, and maybe even all those from my first talk, could be united under the sign of an Olympian I particularly revere: Hermes/Mercury, god of communication and mediation, who under the name of Thoth invented writing, and who as the "Spirit Mercury" also represents, as Carl Jung tells us in his work on alchemical symbolism, the *principium individuationis*—the principle of individuation. Mercury, with wings on his feet, light and airborne, clever and nimble and adaptable and casual, establishes relations between one god and another as well as relations between gods and men, between universal laws and individual cases, between natural forces and cultural forms, between all the world's objects and all its thinking subjects. What better patron could I choose for my literary proposal?

Among the ancients, who saw microcosm and macrocosm mirrored in the correspondences between psychology and astrology (between humors, temperaments, planets, constellations), Mercury's status was highly indefinite and variable. But according to the most widespread opinion, temperaments influenced by Mercury, with their knack for exchange and commerce, contrasted with temperaments influenced by Saturn: gloomy, contemplative, solitary. Since antiquity, saturnine temperaments have been seen as characteristic of artists, poets, and thinkers, and I think there's truth in that view. Certainly literature would never have existed if some human beings had not been given to deep introversion, to dissatisfaction with the world as it is, to forgetting themselves for hours and days, their gaze fixed on mute, unmoving words. Certainly my own character shares some of the conventional traits of my trade: I too have always had a saturnine disposition, whatever other mask I might have tried to wear. Perhaps my devotion to Mercury reveals an aspiration, a desire to be: I am a saturnine man who wants to be mercurial, and everything I write shows traces of both impulses.

But if Saturn/Cronos does have some power over me, it is nonetheless true that I have never been devoted to him; I have never felt anything for him other than respectful fear. There is, though, another god, related to Saturn by affinity and blood, for whom I have great affection, a god who, not having had one of the seven planets of the ancient sky named after him, has not enjoyed as much astrological and therefore psychological prestige but who has on the other hand enjoyed, ever since Homeric times, excellent literary fortunes; I'm speaking of Vulcan/Hephaestus, who doesn't roam the skies but rather holes up in craters, working tirelessly in his smithy to forge objects of great refinement — jewels and ornaments for the gods and goddesses, weapons, shields, nets, traps. In contrast to the soaring flight of Mercury, Vulcan offers his halting gait and his rhythmic hammer.

Here too I must refer to something I happened to read, one of those books that seems, from an academic point of view, strange or hard to categorize but that gives rise to clarifying ideas. The book in question, which I read when I was studying the symbolism of the tarot, is André Virel's *Histoire de notre image* (*History of Our Image*, 1965). According to Virel, a student of the collective imagination in (I believe) the Jungian school, Mercury and Vulcan represent two inseparable and complementary functions of life: Mercury represents *syntony*, or harmonious participation in the world around us; Vulcan represents *focalization*, or constructive concentration. Mercury and Vulcan are both sons of Jupiter, whose realm is that of individual as well as social consciousness. But on his mother's side, Mercury is descended from Uranus, who ruled over the "cyclophrenic" age of undifferentiated continuity, while Vulcan descends from Saturn, who ruled over the "schizophrenic" age of egocentric isolation. Saturn had dethroned Uranus, Jupiter had dethroned Saturn, and in the end, in the stable and resplendent realm of Jupiter, both Mercury and Vulcan bear the memory of dark primordial realms but transform their destructive maladies into positive qualities: syntony and focalization.

When I read Virel's explanation of Mercury and Vulcan as both contrasting and complementary, I began to grasp something I had previously only vaguely intuited—something about myself, about how I am and how I wish to be, about how I write and how I might write. Vulcan's concentration and craftsmanship are necessary in order to write about Mercury's adventures and transformations. Mercury's mobility and swiftness are needed to imbue Vulcan's endless labors with meaning and to shape the shapeless mineral gangue into the attributes of the gods: lyres or tridents, spears or diadems. A writer's labor involves keeping track of different times: Mercury's time and Vulcan's time; a message of spontaneity obtained by means of patient, meticulous adjustments; a flash of insight that immediately takes on the finality of that which was inevitable; and also time that flows for no reason other than to allow feelings and thoughts to settle and ripen, unfettered by any impatience, any fleeting contingency.

I began this talk by telling a story—let me end it with another story, this one Chinese. Among Zhuang Zhou's many virtues was his talent for drawing. The king asked him to draw a crab. Zhuang Zhou said he would need five years and a villa with twelve servants. After five years he had not yet begun the drawing. "I need another five years," he said. The king agreed. When the tenth year was up, Zhuang Zhou took his brush and in an instant, with a single flourish, drew a crab, the most perfect crab anyone had ever seen.

3

Exactitude

Precision, to the ancient Egyptians, was symbolized by the feather that served as counterweight in the scales that weighed souls. That light feather was called Maat, after the goddess of the scales. The hieroglyph for Maat also signified a unit of length (the 33 centimeters of the standard brick) and the fundamental note of the flute.

This news comes from a lecture by Giorgio de Santillana on the precision of ancient astronomical observations, a lecture I heard in Italy in 1963 that had a profound influence on me. I have been thinking a lot about Santillana lately, since it was he who served as my Massachusetts guide the first time I came to this country, in 1960. In memory of his friendship, I begin this lecture on exactitude in literature with Maat, goddess of the scales — all the more because I'm a Libra.

First I will try to define my topic. For me, exactitude means above all three things:

1) a well-defined, well-considered design for the work;

2) the evocation of clear, sharp, memorable images (in Italian we have an adjective that doesn't exist in English: *icastico,* from the Greek εἰκαστικός);

3) a language that is as precise as possible in its choice of words and in its expression of the nuances of thought and imagination.

Why do I feel the need to defend things that many will consider obvious values? My initial impulse derives perhaps from a hypersensitivity or allergy of mine: it seems to me that language is always being used in a loose, haphazard, careless manner, which I find unbearably annoying. But don't think that this reaction is based on intolerance for others; I feel the greatest annoyance when listening to myself. That's why I try to speak as little as possible, and if I prefer to write, it's because when writing I can revise every phrase as many times as necessary, if not to achieve satisfaction with my words, at least to eliminate those reasons I can see for dissatisfaction.

Literature—by which I mean literature that responds to these demands—is the Promised Land in which language becomes what it truly ought to be.

Sometimes it seems to me that a terrible plague has struck humanity in the faculty that most distinguishes it, its use of words—a plague that manifests in language as a loss of cognitive power and immediacy, as an automatic tendency to reduce expression to its most generic, anonymous, abstract constructions and to dilute its meanings, blunt its expressive points, and snuff every spark that flies from the collision of words with new circumstances.

I'm not concerned here with whether the origins of this epidemic can be traced to politics, to ideology, to bureaucratic uniformity, to the homogenization of mass media, or to the diffusion in schools of middlebrow culture. What interests me are the possible remedies. Literature, and perhaps only literature, can create the antibodies that might resist the spread of this language plague.

I hasten to add that it isn't just language that seems to have contracted this plague. Take images, for example. We live beneath a continuous rain of images; the most powerful media do nothing but turn the world into images and multiply it with the kaleidoscopic play of mirrors—images that are largely void of the internal necessity that ought to distinguish every image, as a form and as a meaning, as a force that lays claim to our attention, as a wealth of possible meanings. Much of this cloud of imagery dissolves immediately, like dreams that leave no trace in memory, but a sense of irrelevance and uneasiness remains.

Perhaps this insubstantiality does not reside in images and language alone but in the world. The plague also afflicts the lives of individuals and the histories of nations, rendering all histories formless, haphazard, confused, without beginning or end. My uneasiness is for the loss of form that I perceive in life, against which I try to mount the only defense I am able to imagine: an idea of literature.

I could, then, just as easily use negative terms to define the value I'm proposing to defend. It remains to be seen whether one might also defend the opposite position with equally persuasive arguments. Giacomo Leopardi, for example, claimed that language becomes more poetic as it becomes more vague and imprecise. (I'll mention in passing that Italian is, I believe, the only language in which the word for "vague" (*vago*) also means charming, attractive; having originally meant "wandering," it still carries with it a feeling of movement and mutability, which in Italian suggests not only uncertainty and indeterminacy but also grace and pleasure.)

In order to put my love for exactitude to the test, I'll read over those passages of the *Zibaldone* in which Leopardi praises the vague. He writes:

> *Le parole* lontano, antico *e simili sono poeticissime e piacevoli, perché destano idee vaste, e indefinite . . .*
>
> (25 settembre 1821)
>
> . . .
>
> *Le parole* notte, notturno *ec., le descrizioni della notte sono poeticissime, perché la notte confondendo gli oggetti, l'animo non ne concepisce che un'immagine vaga, indistinta, incompleta, sì di essa che di quanto essa contiene. Così* oscurità, profondo, *ec. ec.*
>
> (28 settembre 1821)

*

Words like *distant* and *ancient* are highly poetic and pleasing, because they awaken vast, indefinite ideas . . .

(September 25, 1821)

. . .

The words *night, nighttime,* etc., descriptions of night, are highly poetic, because night confounds objects so that the mind conceives nothing but a vague, blurred, incomplete image, of both night itself and whatever it contains. Likewise *darkness, deep,* etc.

(September 28, 1821)

Leopardi's poems perfectly illustrate his reasoning, lending it the authority of incontrovertible evidence. Continuing to browse in the *Zibaldone* in search of other examples of this passion of his, I find a longer-than-usual entry—a list of situations suited to the "indefinite" state of mind:

> . . . *la luce del sole o della luna, veduta in luogo dov'essi non si vedano e non si scopra la sorgente della luce; un luogo solamente in parte illuminato da essa luce; il riflesso di detta luce, e i vari effetti materiali che ne derivano; il penetrare di detta luce in luoghi dov'ella divenga incerta e impedita, e non bene si distingua, come attraverso un canneto, in una selva, per li balconi socchiusi ec. ec.; la detta luce veduta in luogo, oggetto ec. dov'ella non entri e non percota dirittamente, ma vi*

*sia ribattuta e diffusa da qualche altro luogo od oggetto
ec. dov'ella venga a battere; in un andito veduto al di
dentro o al di fuori, e in una loggia parimente ec. quei
luoghi dove la luce si confonde ec. ec. colle ombre, come
sotto un portico, in una loggia elevata e pensile, fra le
rupi e i burroni, in una valle, sui colli veduti dalla parte
dell'ombra, in modo che ne sieno indorate le cime; il
riflesso che produce, per esempio, un vetro colorato su
quegli oggetti su cui si riflettono i raggi che passano per
detto vetro; tutti quegli oggetti insomma che per diverse
materiali e menome circostanze giungono alla nostra
vista, udito ec. in modo incerto, mal distinto, imper-
fetto, incompleto, o fuor dell'ordinario ec.*

(20 settembre 1821)

. . . sunlight or moonlight, seen from a place where
neither sun nor moon is visible and the light's
source is unknown; a place only partly lit by this
light; the reflection of such light and the various
material effects that derive from it; the penetration
of such light into places where it becomes uncertain and obstructed and difficult to make out, as
through a canebrake, within a forest, beyond half-
closed shutters, etc.; such light seen in a place, object etc. where it does not enter or strike directly
but has been reflected or diffused by some other
place or object etc. that it does hit; in a narrow

passage seen from within or without, and likewise
in a loggia etc., those places where light mixes etc.
etc. with shadows, as beneath a portico, in a high
jutting balcony, between a bluff and ravine, in a
valley, on hills seen from the shady side when their
peaks are gilded; the reflection made, for example,
by a colored pane of glass on those objects struck
by the rays that pass through the glass; all those
objects in short that due to diverse substances or
minimal conditions reach our sight, hearing etc. in
a manner that is uncertain, indistinct, imperfect,
incomplete, or out of the ordinary etc.

(September 20, 1821)

So this is what Leopardi demands of us if we are to savor
the beauty of the indeterminate and the vague! He pays extremely precise and careful attention to the composition of
each image—to the minute definition of the details, to the
choice of the objects, the lighting, the atmosphere—all in
order to achieve the desired vagueness. So it is that Leopardi,
whom I chose as the ideal refuter of my defense of exactitude,
turns out to be a key witness on its behalf ... The poet of
vagueness can only be the poet of precision, able to capture
the subtlest sensations with quick and reliable eyes and ears
and hands. It is worthwhile to read the end of this entry in
the *Zibaldone;* his meditation on the indeterminate becomes
an observation of all that is manifold, teeming, particulate:

È piacevolissima e sentimentalissima la stessa luce
veduta nelle città, dov'ella è frastagliata dalle ombre,
dove lo scuro contrasta in molti luoghi col chiaro, dove
la luce in molte parti degrada appoco appoco, come sui
tetti, dove alcuni luoghi riposti nascondono la vista
dell'astro luminoso ec. ec. A questo piacere contribuisce
la varietà, l'incertezza, il non veder tutto, e il potersi
perciò spaziare coll'immaginazione, riguardo a ciò che
non si vede. Similmente dico dei simili effetti, che pro-
ducono gli alberi, i filari, i colli, i pergolati, i casolari,
i pagliai, le ineguaglianze del suolo ec. nelle campagne.
Per lo contrario una vasta e tutta uguale pianura, dove
la luce si spazi e diffonda senza diversità, né ostacolo;
dove l'occhio si perda ec. è pure piacevolissima, per
l'idea indefinita in estensione, che deriva da tal veduta.
Così un cielo senza nuvolo. Nel qual proposito osservo
che il piacere della varietà e dell'incertezza prevale a
quello dell'apparente infinità, e dell'immensa unifor-
mità. E quindi un cielo variamente sparso di nuvoletti, è
forse più piacevole di un cielo affatto puro; e la vista del
cielo è forse meno piacevole di quella della terra, e delle
campagne ec. perché meno varia (ed anche meno simile
a noi, meno propria di noi, meno appartenente alle cose
nostre ec.). Infatti, ponetevi supino in modo che voi non
vediate se non il cielo, separato dalla terra, voi proverete
una sensazione molto meno piacevole che considerando
una campagna, o considerando il cielo nella sua corris-

*pondenza e relazione colla terra, ed unitamente ad essa
in un medesimo punto di vista.*

*È piacevolissima ancora, per le sopraddette cagioni,
la vista di una moltitudine innumerabile, come delle
stelle, o di persone ec. un moto moltiplice, incerto, con-
fuso, irregolare, disordinato, un ondeggiamento vago
ec., che l'animo non possa determinare, né concepire
definitamente e distintamente ec., come quello di una
folla, o di un gran numero di formiche o del mare agi-
tato ec. Similmente una moltitudine di suoni irregolar-
mente mescolati, e non distinguibili l'uno dall'altro ec.
ec. ec.*

(20 settembre 1821)

It is highly pleasing and very moving to see the
same light in cities, where it is notched with shadows, where darkness in many places vies with
brightness, where light in many areas gradually
degrades, as above the roofs, where some secluded
places block the luminous star from view etc. etc.
Contributing to this pleasure are the variety, the
uncertainty, the inability to see everything, and
hence the ability to wander with one's imagination where one cannot see. I say similar things
about similar effects produced by trees, vineyards,
hills, pergolas, cottages, haystacks, uneven ground
etc. in the countryside. Conversely a vast and level

plain, where light spreads and diffuses, unchanging and unchecked, where the eye loses itself etc. is also highly pleasing, because of the idea of indefinite extension suggested by such a view. Likewise a cloudless sky. In this regard I note that the pleasure of variety and uncertainty is greater than that of apparent infinity and immense uniformity. And hence a sky scattered with little clouds is perhaps more pleasurable than a totally clear sky; and a view of the sky is perhaps less pleasurable than one of the land, the countryside etc. because less various (and also less like us, less suited to us, less related to what is ours etc.). Indeed, if you lie on your back so that you can see only sky, cut off from the land, the sensation you feel will be much less pleasing than looking at a landscape, or at the sky as it corresponds and relates to the land, joined with it in a single view.

Also highly pleasing, for the above reasons, is the sight of a countless multitude, as of stars, or people etc., a multifarious, indistinct, confused, irregular, disorderly motion, a vague undulation etc. that the mind cannot fix nor definitely and distinctly grasp etc., as with a crowd, or a great number of ants or rough seas etc. Likewise a multitude of mixed irregular sounds, indistinguishable one from the other etc. etc. etc.

(September 20, 1821)

Here we come to one of the cruxes of Leopardi's poetics, and the crux of his loveliest and most famous lyric, "L'infinito" ("The Infinite"). Shielded by a hedge beyond which he sees only the sky, the poet feels both fear and pleasure at the thought of infinite spaces. The poem is from 1819; the *Zibaldone* entry I just quoted is from two years later, showing that Leopardi was still reflecting on the questions raised by the writing of "L'infinito." In his reflections, two terms are repeatedly contrasted: *indefinite* and *infinite*. For Leopardi, unhappy hedonist that he was, the unknown is always more appealing than the known; hope and imagination are the only consolations for the disappointments and sorrows of experience. Man thus projects his desire onto the infinite, feeling pleasure only when he can imagine that it won't end. But since the human brain can't grasp the infinite, indeed recoils in fear from the very thought, it must content itself with the indefinite, with sensations that as they blur together create an impression of boundlessness, illusory but still pleasing. It isn't only in the poem's famous last line— *"E il naufragar m'è dolce in questo mare"* (And sweet to me is shipwreck in this sea) —that sweetness overcomes fear, because the music of the lines always conveys a sense of sweetness, even when they are describing painful experiences.

I realize that I'm reading Leopardi only in terms of sensations, as if I accepted the image he means to give of himself as a devotee of eighteenth-century sensism. In fact, the problem he is tackling is speculative and metaphysical, a problem central to the history of philosophy from Parmenides to Descartes and Kant: the relation between, on one hand, the idea of the infinite as absolute space and absolute time, and on the other, our empirical perception of space and time. Leopardi thus begins with the abstract rigor of a mathematical idea of space and time, which he then sets against the vague, indefinite flux of sensations.

In Robert Musil's endless and indeed unfinished novel *Der Mann ohne Eigenschaften* (*The Man Without Qualities*), exactitude and indeterminacy are also the poles between which waver the ironic philosophical conjectures of the protagonist, Ulrich.

> *Ist nun das beobachtete Element die Exaktheit selbst, hebt man es heraus und lässt es sich entwickeln, betrachtet man es als Denkgewohnheit und Lebenshaltung und lässt es seine beispielgebende Kraft auf alles auswirken, was mit ihm in Berührung kommt, so wird man zu einem Menschen geführt, in dem eine paradoxe Verbindung von Genauigkeit und Unbestimmtheit stattfindet. Er besitzt jene unbestechliche gewollte Kaltblütigkeit, die das Temperament der Exaktheit darstellt; über diese Eigenschaft hinaus ist aber alles andere unbestimmt.*

> If, now, the element under observation is exactitude itself, if one isolates it and allows it to de-

velop, if one regards it as an intellectual habit
and a way of living and lets it exert its exemplary
influence on everything that comes into contact
with it, the logical conclusion is a human being
in whom there is a paradoxical combination of
precision and indefiniteness. He possesses that
incorruptible, deliberate cold-bloodedness, the
temperament that goes with exactitude; but
apart from and beyond this quality all is indefinite.

(trans. by Eithne Wilkins and Ernst Kaiser)

Musil comes closest to proposing a solution when, in chapter
83, he recalls the existence of "mathematical problems that
did not admit of any general solution, though they did admit
of particular solutions, the combining of which brought one
nearer to the general solution," (*mathematischen Aufgaben, die
keine allgemeine Lösung zulassen, wohl aber Einzellösungen, durch
deren Kombination man sich der allgemeinen Lösung nähert*) and
he believes that this method could be adapted to human life.
Many years later, in *La chambre claire* (*Camera Lucida*), Roland
Barthes, another writer in whose mind the demons of exactitude and sensitivity cohabited, wondered whether it was
possible to imagine a science of the unique and unrepeat-
able: "Why couldn't there be, somehow, a new science for
each object? A *mathesis singularis* (and no longer *universalis*)?"
(*Pourquoi n'y aurait-il pas, en quelque sorte, une science nouvelle
par objet? Une* Mathesis singularis *[et non plus* universalis*]?*)

If Musil's Ulrich soon resigns himself to the defeats that a passion for exactitude inevitably entails, Paul Valéry's Monsieur Teste, another of the century's great intellectual characters, never doubts the fact that the human spirit can be fulfilled in the most precise and rigorous way. And if Leopardi, poet of life's pain, displays supreme precision in evoking indefinite sensations that cause pleasure, Valéry, poet of the mind's impassive rigor, displays supreme precision in having his Monsieur Teste confront pain, making him fight against physical suffering by means of an exercise in geometric abstraction.

> "J'ai, dit-il, ... pas grand'chose. J'ai ... un dixième de seconde qui se montre ... Attendez ... Il y a des instants où mon corps s'illumine ... C'est très curieux. J'y vois tout à coup en moi ... je distingue les profondeurs des couches de ma chair; et je sens des zones de douleur, des anneaux, des pôles, des aigrettes de douleur. Voyez-vous ces figures vives? cette géométrie de ma souffrance? Il y a de ces éclairs qui ressemblent tout à fait à des idées. Ils font comprendre, —d'ici, jusque-là ... Et pourtant ils me laissent incertain. Incertain n'est pas le mot ... Quand cela va venir, je trouve en moi quelque chose de confus ou de diffus. Il se fait dans mon être des endroits ... brumeux, il y a des étendues qui font leur apparition. Alors, je prends dans ma mémoire une question, un problème quelconque ... Je m'y enfonce. Je compte des grains de sable ... et, tant

*que je les vois . . . —Ma douleur grossissante me force
à l'observer. J'y pense! —Je n'attends que mon cri, . . .
et dès que je l'ai entendu —l'objet, le terrible objet,
devenant plus petit, et encore plus petit, se dérobe à ma
vue intérieure . . ."*

"It's nothing . . . much," he said. "It's . . . a tenth
of a second appearing . . . Wait . . . At certain moments my body lights up . . . This is very odd. Suddenly I can see into myself . . . I can make out the
depths of the layers of my flesh; I feel zones of pain
. . . rings, poles, plumes of pain. Do you see these
living forms, this geometry of my suffering? There
are certain flashes that are exactly like ideas. They
make me understand —from here, to there . . . Yet
they leave me uncertain. *Uncertain* is not the word
. . . When *it* is coming on, I find something confused or diffused in me. Inside my *self* . . . foggy
places arise, there are open expanses that come
into view. Then I pick out a question from my
memory, some problem or other . . . and plunge
into it. I count grains of sand . . . and so long as I
can see them . . . My increasing pain forces me to
notice it. I think about it! Waiting only to hear my
cry . . . and the moment I hear it, the *object,* the terrible *object,* smaller and still smaller, vanishes from
my inner sight . . ."

(trans. by Jackson Mathews)

In our century, it was Valéry who best defined poetry as a striving toward exactitude. I'm speaking mainly of his work as a critic and essayist, in which the poetics of exactitude are traced back through Mallarmé to Baudelaire and from Baudelaire to Poe.

In Poe—the Poe of Baudelaire and of Mallarmé—Valéry sees "the demon of lucidity, the genius of analysis and the inventor of the most novel and seductive combinations of logic and imagination, of mysticism and math; the psychologist of the exceptional, the literary engineer who studies and uses all the resources of his art" (*le démon de la lucidité, le génie de l'analyse et l'inventeur des combinaisons les plus neuves et les plus séduisantes de la logique avec l'imagination, de la mysticité avec le calcul, le psycologue de l'exception, l'ingénieur littéraire qui approfondit et utilise toutes les ressources de l'art*). So says Valéry in his essay "Situation de Baudelaire" ("Baudelaire's Situation"), which for me has the value of a poetic manifesto, together with another essay of his, on Poe's *Eureka* and cosmogony.

In the *Eureka* essay, Valéry ruminates on cosmogony as a literary genre rather than as a branch of science, and he produces a brilliant refutation of the idea of a universe, a refutation that is also an affirmation of the mythic power that every image of a universe carries with it. Here, as in Leopardi, the infinite as both attractive and repellent . . . Here too cosmological speculations as literary genre, which Leopardi indulged in with some of his prose "apocrypha"—such as his "Frammento apocrifo di Stratone da Lampsaco" ("Apocryphal Fragment of Strato of Lampsacus"), on the origin and especially the end of our world, which flattens and empties like the rings of Saturn and disperses until it burns up in the sun. Or his apocryphal Talmudic text, "Cantico del gallo silvestre" ("Song of the Wild Rooster"), where it's the whole universe that gets extinguished and disappears: ". . . a naked silence, and a profound stillness, will fill the immense space. And thus the marvelous and frightening mystery of universal existence, before it can be uttered or understood, will fade and be lost" (. . . *un silenzio nudo, e una quiete altissima, empieranno lo spazio immenso. Così questo arcano mirabile e spaventoso dell'esistenza universale, innanzi di essere dichiarato né inteso, si dileguerà e perderassi*). It is not the infinite here that is frightening and inconceivable but rather existence.

This talk is refusing to be led in the direction I meant to go. I set out to speak about exactitude, not infinity or the cosmos. I wanted to tell you about my fondness for geometric forms, for symmetries and sequences, for combinatorics, for numerical proportions—to explain what I've written in terms of my fidelity to the idea of limits, of measure . . . But perhaps it is that very idea that evokes what is endless: the succession of whole numbers, the straight lines of Euclid . . . Rather than telling you how I've written what I've written, perhaps it would be more interesting to tell you about problems I have yet to resolve and don't know how to resolve, about what they might spur me to write . . . Sometimes when I try to concentrate on a story I'd like to write, I realize that what interests me is some other thing, or rather not something specific but everything that gets left out of what I'm supposed to be writing: the relation between that given argument and all its possible variants and alternatives, all the incidents that time and space can contain. It is a voracious, destructive obsession, which can block me from writing. To fight it, I try to limit the field of what I have to say, then divide it into even smaller fields, then subdivide those, and so on. And then I'm seized by another kind of vertigo, that of the detail of the detail of the detail: I get sucked into the infinitesimal, the infinitely small, when I was previously lost in the infinitely vast.

Flaubert says that "the good God is in the details," a statement I'd like to explain in light of the philosophy of Giordano Bruno, that great visionary cosmologist who sees the universe as infinite and composed of countless worlds. He won't call it "totally infinite," however, because each of those worlds is finite. God, on the other hand, is "totally infinite," because "all of him is in all the world, and in each of its parts infinitely and totally."

In recent years the Italian book that I have read, reread, and meditated on the most is Paolo Zellini's *Breve storia dell'infinito* (*A Brief History of Infinity*, 1980), which opens with Borges's famous attack on the infinite—"a concept that corrupts and deranges all the others" (*un concepto que es el corruptor y el desatinador de los otros*)—then goes on to review the many arguments on the subject, and ends up by dissolving and reversing the expanse of the infinite into the density of the infinitesimal.

I believe that this link between the formal choices of literary composition and the need for a cosmological model (or at least a general mythological framework) is present even for authors who do not explicitly declare it. The taste for geometrizing composition, whose history in world literature might be traced back to Mallarmé, is rooted in the opposition, so fundamental to contemporary science, between order and disorder. The universe dissolves into a cloud of heat, it plummets helplessly into a maelstrom of entropy — but within this irreversible process there may appear zones of order, portions of the existent that tend toward a shape, privileged points from which one may discern a design, a perspective. The literary work is one of these tiny portions in which the existent crystallizes into a shape, acquires a meaning — not fixed, not definitive, not hardened into mineral immobility, but alive, like an organism. Poetry is the great enemy of chance, despite also being a daughter of chance and despite knowing that chance in the end will triumph: "No throw of the dice," writes Mallarmé, "will ever abolish chance" (*Un coup de dés jamais n'abolira le hasard*).

It is in this context that we ought to view the reexamination of logical, geometrical, and metaphysical techniques that became popular in the visual arts in the early decades of the century and later in literature. The emblem of the crystal might serve to identify a highly diverse constellation of poets and writers, including Paul Valéry in France, Wallace Stevens in America, Gottfried Benn in Germany, Fernando Pessoa in Portugal, Ramón Gómez de la Serna in Spain, Massimo Bontempelli in Italy, and Jorge Luis Borges in Argentina.

The crystal, with its precise facets and its ability to refract light, is a model of perfection that I've always taken as an emblem, and its appeal became even stronger for me when it was discovered that certain aspects of the birth and growth of crystals resemble those of rudimentary biological creatures, making crystals a sort of bridge between the mineral world and living matter.

Recently, in one of the scientific books I sometimes flip through in an effort to spur my imagination, I happened to read that the models for the formation process of living creatures are "the *crystal* on the one side (invariance of specific structures) and the *flame* on the other (constancy of external forms in spite of relentless internal agitation)." I'm quoting from Massimo Piattelli-Palmarini's introduction to *Language and Learning: The Debate between Jean Piaget and Noam Chomsky* (1980). The contrasting images of flame and crystal are used to illustrate the alternatives offered to biology, before moving on from there to theories of language and learning ability. I'll leave aside the implications for the philosophy of science of the positions of Piaget, who favors the principle of "order from noise"—the flame—and Chomsky, who favors the "self-organizing system"—the crystal.

What interests me here is the juxtaposition of these two images, as in one of those sixteenth-century emblems I mentioned in my previous talk. Crystal and flame, two forms of perfect beauty that rivet the gaze, two modes of growth over time, of use of surrounding material, two moral symbols, two absolutes, two categories for classifying facts and ideas and styles and feelings. A little while ago I referred to a crystal faction in the literature of our century; no doubt a matching list could be drawn up for the flame faction. I've always been a partisan of crystals, but the passage I just quoted reminds me of the value of flame as a way of being, as a form of existence. Similarly, I would hope that the followers of flame won't forget the calm, difficult lesson of crystals.

A more complex symbol, one that gave me the greatest opportunity to express the tension between geometric rationality and the tangle of human lives, is that of the city. The book in which I think I've had the most to say remains *Invisible Cities*, because I was able to focus all my reflections and experiences and conjectures on a single symbol. And also because I created a multifaceted structure in which each brief text sits close to others in a sequence that doesn't suggest causality or hierarchy but rather a network within which one can follow multiple paths and come to various ramified conclusions.

In *Invisible Cities* every concept and every value—even exactitude—turns out to be double. Kublai Khan at a certain point personifies the intellect's rationalizing, geometrizing, algebrizing tendency, reducing knowledge of his empire to the permutations of pieces on a chessboard. The cities Marco Polo describes to Khan in such great detail are represented by Khan with different arrangements of castles, bishops, knights, kings, queens, and pawns, all on black and white squares. This operation leads him to the ultimate conclusion that the object of his conquests is nothing more than the wooden square on which each piece rests: an emblem of nothingness . . . But then comes a dramatic turn: Marco Polo invites the Great Khan to look more closely at what he sees as nothingness.

Il Gran Khan cercava d'immedesimarsi nel gioco: ma adesso era il perché del gioco a sfuggirgli. Il fine d'ogni partita è una vincita o una perdita: ma di cosa? Qual era la vera posta? Allo scacco matto, sotto il piede del re sbalzato via dalla mano del vincitore, resta il nulla: un quadrato nero o bianco. A forza di scorporare le sue conquiste per ridurle all'essenza, Kublai era arrivato all'operazione estrema: la conquista definitiva, di cui i multiformi tesori dell'impero non erano che involucri illusori, si riduceva a un tassello di legno piallato.

Allora Marco Polo parlò:—La tua scacchiera, sire, è un intarsio di due legni: ebano e acero. Il tassello sul quale si fissa il tuo sguardo illuminato fu tagliato in uno strato del tronco che crebbe in un anno di siccità: vedi come si dispongono le fibre? Qui si scorge un nodo appena accennato: una gemma tentò di spuntare in un giorno di primavera precoce, ma la brina della notte l'obbligò a desistere—.

Il Gran Khan non s'era fin'allora reso conto che lo

straniero sapesse esprimersi fluentemente nella sua lingua, ma non era questo a stupirlo.

—Ecco un poro più grosso: forse è stato il nido d'una larva; non d'un tarlo, perché appena nato avrebbe continuato a scavare, ma d'un bruco che rosicchiò le foglie e fu la causa per cui l'albero fu scelto per essere abbattuto . . . Questo margine fu inciso dall'ebanista con la sgorbia perché aderisse al quadrato vicino, più sporgente . . .

La quantità di cose che si potevano leggere in un pezzetto di legno liscio e vuoto sommergeva Kublai; già Polo era venuto a parlare dei boschi d'ebano, delle zattere di tronchi che discendono i fiumi, degli approdi, delle donne alle finestre . . .

The Great Khan tried to immerse himself in the game, but now it was the point of the game that escaped him. Every match ends with a win or a loss—but of what? What was really at stake? At checkmate, what's left in place of the king, flung aside by the winner's hand, is nothingness: a black or white square. By dint of abstracting his conquests to reduce them to their essence, Kublai had arrived at the final operation; the definitive conquest, of which the empire's multifarious treasures were but illusory husks, came down to a tile of planed wood.

Then Marco Polo spoke: "Your chessboard, sire,

is an inlay of two woods: ebony and maple. The tile on which your enlightened gaze is fixed was cut from the cross-section of a trunk that grew in a year of drought; do you see how the fibers are arranged? Here we can make out the faint hint of a knot: a bud tried to sprout one day in early spring, but the night's frost obliged it to desist."

The Great Khan had not realized until then that the foreigner could express himself fluently in his language, but that wasn't what amazed him.

"Here is a larger pore; perhaps it was the nest of a larva. Not a woodworm, which would have continued digging after it was born, but a caterpillar that nibbled on leaves and was the reason the tree was chosen to be felled . . . This edge was trimmed by the woodworker with a gouge so as to fit flush against the square beside it, which bulges . . ."

That so much could be read in a bit of smooth and empty wood overwhelmed Kublai. Now Polo was speaking about forests of ebony, about rafts of timber floating down rivers, about landings, about women at their windows . . .

As soon as I wrote that page, it became clear to me that my pursuit of exactitude was forking in two directions: on one hand, the reduction of incidental events to abstract schemes that could be used to perform operations and demonstrate theorems; on the other, the effort of words to convey as precisely as possible the perceptible aspect of things.

Indeed my writing has always found itself facing two divergent roads that correspond to two kinds of knowledge: one that moves through mental spaces of disembodied rationality, in which lines can be drawn that connect points, projections, abstract shapes, vectors of force; another that moves in a space crowded with objects and seeks to create a verbal equivalent of that space by filling pages with words, in a meticulous effort to match the written to the not-written, to the sum of the sayable and the not-sayable. These are two distinct drives toward exactitude that will never reach absolute fulfillment: the first because natural languages always say something *more* than formalized languages—they always carry a certain amount of noise that alters the essence of the information; and the second because in trying to account for the density and continuity of the world around us, language is exposed as lacunose, fragmentary: it always says something *less* than the sum of what can be experienced.

I constantly go back and forth between these two roads, and when I feel that I have fully explored the possibilities of one, I head over to the other, and vice versa. So it is that in recent years I have alternated my exercises on the structure of the story with exercises of description (an art nowadays much neglected). Like a schoolboy whose homework assignment is to "describe a giraffe" or "describe a starry sky," I applied myself to filling a notebook with such exercises and then made a book out of them. The book is called *Palomar* and has just come out as *Mr. Palomar* in English translation: it's a kind of diary of minimal problems of knowledge, of ways of establishing relations with the world, of satisfactions and frustrations in the use of silence and language.

In this line of inquiry, I have kept in mind the experience of poets. I think of William Carlos Williams, who describes cyclamen leaves in such minute detail that he causes the flower to take shape and bloom from the leaves he has described and so succeeds in giving to the poem the lightness of the plant. I think of Marianne Moore, who in depicting her pangolin and her nautilus and all the other creatures of her bestiary imbues information from zoology books with symbolic and allegorical significance, making each of her poems a moral fable. I think of Eugenio Montale, who might be said to combine both effects in his poem "L'anguilla" ("The Eel"), which consists of a single very long sentence that takes the form of an eel, traces its entire life, and makes it into a moral symbol.

But above all I think of Francis Ponge, who with his little prose poems created a genre unique in contemporary literature: that very "exercise book" of the schoolboy who must first of all practice applying his words to the range of the world's features, which he does with a series of attempts, rough drafts, approximations. For me Ponge is a peerless master, because when his brief texts—in *Le parti pris des choses* (*The Nature of Things*, 1942) and other similar collections— speak of a shrimp (*"La crevette"*) or a pebble (*"Le galet"*) or a bar of soap (*"Le savon"*), they represent the best example of the struggle to force language to become the language of things, to start with things and come back to us laden with everything human we have invested in things. Ponge's declared intention was to compose, by means of his brief texts and their elaborate variations, a new *De rerum natura*, and I think we can regard him as the Lucretius of our times, one who reconstructs the physical nature of the world with the impalpable powder of words.

It seems to me that Ponge works the same field as Mallarmé, though in a different, complementary direction: in Mallarmé, language achieves extreme precision by approaching the limit of abstraction and identifying nothingness as the world's ultimate substance; in Ponge, the world takes the form of the most humble, incidental, lopsided things, and words are what serve to give an account of the infinite variety of these irregular and minutely complex forms. There are those who believe that words are the means of getting at the world's substance — its ultimate, unique, absolute substance; that rather than representing that substance, words become it (it is therefore mistaken to call them a *means*): the word knows only itself, and no other knowledge of the world is possible. Then there are those who see the use of words as a never-ending pursuit of things, an approximation not of their substance but of their infinite variety, a brushing against their manifold inexhaustible surfaces. As Hofmannsthal said, "Depth must be hidden. Where? On the surface" (*Die Tiefe muß man verstecken.*

Wo? An der Oberfläche). And Wittgenstein went even further: "What is hidden . . . is of no interest to us" (*Was . . . verborgen ist, interessiert uns nicht*).

I don't take such a drastic view: I think we are always hunting something that is hidden or merely possible or hypothetical, something whose tracks we follow as we find them on the surface of the ground. I think our basic mental processes originated in the Paleolithic with our hunter-gatherer forefathers and were handed down through every culture in human history. Words connect the visible track to the invisible thing, the absent thing, the thing that is desired or feared, like a fragile makeshift bridge cast across the void. For this reason the proper use of language, to me, is one that helps us approach things (present or absent) with discretion, attention, and caution, and with respect for what these things (present or absent) can tell us without words.

A profound example of the struggle with language to capture something that nonetheless eludes expression is offered by Leonardo da Vinci. His codices are an extraordinary record of his attempt to express himself more richly, subtly, and precisely in a language that is prickly and knotty. The various stages of the treatment of an idea—which Ponge would publish one after the other, since the true work consists not in its definitive form but in the series of attempts to reach that form—were for Leonardo-the-writer proof of the energy he invested in writing as a cognitive tool and of the fact that, with all the books he planned to write, he was more interested in the process of inquiry than in the completion of a text for publication. Leonardo's subjects too are sometimes similar to Ponge's, as in his series of short fables about objects and animals.

Let's take as an example his fire fable. Leonardo gives a quick summary (fire, offended because the water in the pot is above him even though he is the "superior element" [*superiore elemento*], raises his flames so high that the water boils, overflows, and douses him), which he then develops in three successive drafts, all unfinished, three parallel columns, each time adding some detail, describing how the flame wafts up from a tiny ember, crackling and flaring, through gaps in the logs—but soon he breaks off, as if realizing that there is no limit to how meticulously even the simplest story might be told. Even a tale about a log burning in a kitchen fireplace could expand from within until it becomes infinite.

Leonardo—"an unlettered man" (*omo sanza lettere*), as he called himself—had a difficult relationship with the written word. His knowledge was unmatched in the world, but his ignorance of Latin and of grammar hindered him from communicating in writing with the learned men of his time. Certainly he felt that much of his science could be conveyed better in drawings than in words. (From one of his anatomy notebooks: "O writer, with what letters will you write the total figuration with such perfection as drawing gives us here?" [*O scrittore, con quali lettere scriverai tu con tal perfezione la intera figurazione qual fa qui il disegno?*]) And not only his science: he was also sure that his philosophy could be communicated better by paintings and drawings. But still he felt a constant urge to write, to use writing to investigate the world's secrets and its multifarious manifestations, and to give shape to his imaginings, his emotions, his resentments —as when he inveighs against men of letters, who in his view could merely repeat what they read in other people's books, in contrast with those like himself who were among the "inventors and interpreters between nature and men" (*inventori e interpreti tra la natura e li omini*). And so he wrote more and more: as the years passed he stopped painting and thought by writing or drawing, as if pursuing a single train of thought with drawings and words, filling notebooks with his left-handed mirror writing.

On folio 265 of his Codex Atlanticus, Leonardo begins noting down evidence to support the theory that the earth is growing. After citing examples of buried cities swallowed by the earth, he moves on to fossils of marine animals found in the mountains, and in particular to certain bones that belonged, he supposes, to an antediluvian sea monster. At that moment a vision of the huge creature as it swam through the waves seems to take hold of his imagination; in any case, he flips the page and tries to describe an image of it, three times attempting to capture in a sentence the wonder of his vision:

> *O quante volte fusti tu veduto in fra l'onde del gonfiato*
> *e grande oceano, col setoluto e nero dosso, a guisa di*
> *montagna e con grave e superbo andamento!*

*

O how often were you seen amid the waves of the vast and swollen ocean, with your black and bristling back, like a mountain, with your solemn, stately bearing!

Then he tries to animate the *movement* of the monster, introducing the verb *volteggiare* ("to vault"):

E spesse volte eri veduto in fra l'onde del gonfiato e grande oceano, e col superbo e grave moto gir volteggiando in fra le marine acque. E con setoluto e nero dosso, a guisa di montagna, quelle vincere e sopraffare!

And often were you seen amid the waves of the vast and swollen ocean, vaulting in your stately, solemn fashion through its waters. And with your black and bristling back, like a mountain, defeating and subduing them!

But then he thinks that *volteggiare* might weaken the impression of grandeur and majesty that he's trying to evoke. So he chooses the verb *solcare* ("to plow") and improves the whole construction of the passage, giving it density and rhythm, with assured literary instincts:

O quante volte fusti tu veduto in fra l'onde del gonfiato e grande oceano, a guisa di montagna quelle vincere e

*sopraffare, e col setoluto e nero dosso solcare le marine
acque, e con superbo e grave andamento!*

O how often were you seen amid the waves of the
vast and swollen ocean, like a mountain defeating
and subduing them, and your black and bristling
back plowing through the waters, and your stately,
solemn bearing!

His pursuit of this apparition, which becomes something like a symbol of the solemn power of nature, gives
us a glimpse into the workings of Leonardo's imagination.
I'll end my talk by leaving you with that image, so that you
might preserve it for as long as possible in your memory in all
its clarity and mystery.

4

Visibility

In the *Purgatorio* (XVII, 25), Dante describes a series of images that "rained into my high imagination" (*piovve dentro a l'alta fantasia*). My talk this evening takes its cue from that statement: the imagination is a place in which it rains.

Let's look at the context of this line. We're in Purgatory, on the level of the Wrathful, and Dante is contemplating images that are forming directly in his mind and that represent classical and biblical instances of punished wrath. He understands that these images are raining down from heaven—being sent to him, that is, by God.

On the various levels of Purgatory, besides details of the landscape and of the heavenly sky, besides encounters with the souls of repentant sinners and with supernatural beings, Dante sees scenes that are like quotations or representations of exemplary sins and virtues: first in the form of bas-reliefs that seem to move and speak, then as visions projected before his eyes or voices that reach his ears, and finally as purely mental images. These visions, in short, become ever more interior, as if Dante realized there was no need to invent a new form of meta-representation for each new circle, that he might as well place the visions directly in his mind, without having them pass through his senses.

But before doing that, Dante must define the imagination, which he does in two tercets (XVII, 13–18), with a question and an answer:

> *O imaginativa che ne rube*
> *talvolta sì di fuor, ch'om non s'accorge*
> *perché dintorno suonin mille tube,*
>
> *chi move te, se 'l senso non ti porge?*
> *Moveti lume che nel ciel s'informa*
> *per sé o per voler che giù lo scorge.*
>
> O Imagination, you who steal men so
> From outer things that they would miss the sound
> Should in their ears a thousand trumpets blow,
>
> What moves you then, when all the senses drown?
> A light moves you, that finds its form in heaven,
> By itself, or by the will that guides it down.

We're dealing here, of course — as he makes explicit in line 25 — with the "high imagination," that is, with the nobler part of the imagination, as distinct from the corporeal imagination, such as reveals itself in the chaos of dreams. With that point in mind, we can try to follow Dante's thinking, which faithfully reproduces that of the philosophy of his time. I will paraphrase the question:

> O Imagination, you who have the power to impose yourself on our faculties and our wills and to snatch us from the outer world and spirit us away to an inner world, so that even if a thousand trumpets blew we would not hear them, where do the visual messages that you receive originate, when they are not formed by sensations deposited into memory?

The answer: "A light moves you, which finds its form in heaven" (*Moveti lume che nel ciel s'informa*). According to Dante (and Thomas Aquinas), there is a kind of light source in heaven that transmits ideal images, each of which is formed either according to the intrinsic logic of the imaginary world — "by itself" (*per sé*) — or according to the will of God: "or by the will that guides it down" (*o per voler che giù lo scorge*).

Dante is speaking of the visions that appear to him — to Dante the character — almost like movie projections or television broadcasts on a screen that is separate from what for him is the objective reality of his superterranean journey. But for Dante the poet, the entire journey of Dante the character is like these visions. The poet must imagine visually both what his character sees and what he thinks he sees — what he dreams, what he remembers, what he sees represented, what he hears described—just as he must imagine the visual content of the metaphors he uses to facilitate this visual evocation. Dante is attempting, that is, to define the role of imagination in the *Divine Comedy,* and specifically that of the visual aspect of imagination, which precedes or coincides with its verbal aspect.

We can distinguish two types of imaginative processes: one that begins with words and ends with the visual image, and another that begins with the visual image and ends with its verbal expression. The first process is the most common in reading; when we read, for example, a scene in a novel or a story in a newspaper, we are led (to a greater or lesser degree, depending on how effective the text is) to see the scene, or at least those fragments and details of it that emerge from the indistinct, as if it were unfolding before our eyes.

With movies, the image we see on the screen was also filtered through a written text, then "visualized" by the director, then physically reconstructed on the set before being definitively fixed in the frames of the film. A film is therefore the result of a series of stages, physical and nonphysical, through which the images take shape. In this process the role of the imagination's "mental cinema" is no less vital than that of the stages of actual production of the sequences as they are recorded by the camera and then edited on the Moviola. This "mental cinema" is always at work in all of us—and always has been, even before the invention of the cinema—and it never stops projecting images to our inner sight.

It's notable how important the visual imagination becomes in Ignatius of Loyola's *Ejercicios espirituales* (*Spiritual Exercises*). At the very beginning of his manual, Saint Ignatius prescribes "composition by seeing the place" (*composición viendo el lugar*) in terms that read like instructions for the staging of a show:

> . . . *en la contemplación o meditación visible, así como contemplar a Cristo nuestro Señor, el qual es visible, la composición será ver con la vista de la imaginación el lugar corpóreo donde se halla la cosa que quiero contemplar. Digo el lugar corpóreo, así como un templo o monte, donde se halla Jesucristo o nuestra Señora.*

> . . . in a visual contemplation or meditation, such as a contemplation of Christ our Lord, Who is visible, the composition will consist in seeing with the imagination's sight a physical place where the thing I wish to contemplate may be found. I mean a physical place, such as a temple or mount, where Jesus Christ or Our Lady may be found.

Ignatius then hastens to add that the contemplation of one's own sins should not be visual, or rather—if I understand correctly—should be visual only in a metaphorical way (the soul imprisoned in the corruptible body).

Later, on the first day of the second week, the spiritual exercise begins with a sweeping visionary panorama and spectacular crowd scenes:

1er puncto. El primer puncto es ver las personas, las unas y las otras; y primero las de la haz de la tierra, en tanta diversidad, asì en trajes como en gestos, unos blancos y otros negros, unos en paz y otros en guerra, unos llorando y otros riendo, unos sanos, otros enfermos, unos nasciendo y otros muriendo, etc.

2e: ver y considerar las tres personas divinas, como en el su solio real o trono de la su divina majestad, còmo miran toda la haz y redondez de la tierra y todas las gentes en tanta çeguedad, y còmo mueren y descienden al infierno.

1st point. The first point is to see the people, this kind and that kind, and first of all those upon the surface of the earth, in all their diversity, both of dress and of manner, some white and others black, some at peace and others at war, some crying and others laughing, some healthy, others sick, some being born and others dying, etc.

2nd: to see and consider the three divine persons, as if on their royal seat or throne of their divine majesty, as they gaze on all the surface and roundness of the world and all its peoples in all their blindness, as they die and go down to hell.

The idea that the God of Moses might not tolerate being represented in images never seems to occur to Ignatius. On the contrary, it's as if he's claiming for every Christian the great visionary gift of Dante and Michelangelo—without even the curb that Dante feels obliged to place on his own figurative imagination when faced with supreme celestial visions of Paradise.

In the following day's spiritual exercise (second meditation), the person meditating must put himself into the scene, assuming the role of actor in the imaginary action:

> *El primer puncto es ver las personas, es a saber, ver a Nuestra Señora y a Josef y a la ancila y al niño Jesús, después de ser nacido, haciéndome yo un pobrecito y esclavito indigno, mirándolos, contemplándolos, y sirviéndolos, en sus necesidades, como si presente me hallase, con todo acatamiento y reverencia posible; y después reflectir en mí mismo para sacar algún provecho.*

> The first point is to see the people, namely Our Lady and Joseph and the handmaid and the Child Jesus after he is born, and to make myself into a wretch, a lowly little slave, gazing upon them, contemplating them, and serving them in their needs, as if I were present there, with utter devotion and reverence, and then to reflect upon myself in order to gain some benefit.

For Counter-Reformation Catholicism, of course, visual communication was a fundamental tool, with the emotions inspired by sacred art serving to lead the believer back toward the meanings taught orally by the Church. But this always required beginning with a given image, one offered by the Church itself rather than "imagined" by the believer. What I think sets Loyola's procedure apart, even with respect to the forms of devotion of his own time, is the shift from word to image as the path to understanding profound meanings. Here too the beginning and end points are already established, but between them lies a field in which individuals can apply their imaginations in an endless variety of ways to the depiction of characters, places, and scenes in motion. The believer himself is called upon to paint frescoes crowded with figures on the walls of his mind, beginning with whatever his visual imagination manages to elicit from a theological pronouncement or a brief verse from the Gospels.

Returning to literary problems, let's ask ourselves how the imagination takes shape in a period when literature no longer looks to some authority or tradition for its origin or its purpose but aims rather for novelty, originality, invention. It seems to me that in that case the question of which comes first, the visual image or the verbal expression (which is a little like the question of the chicken or the egg) leans strongly toward the side of the image.

Where do the images in our imagination "rain" from? Dante, who rightly had a high opinion of himself, did not hesitate to proclaim the direct divine inspiration of his visions. Writers closer to us (with the rare exception of those with a prophetic bent) make their connections to earthly transmitters—to the individual or collective unconscious, for example, or to time regained through sensations that rise up from lost time, or to epiphanies or concentrations of being in a single point or moment. In short, it's a question of processes that, though they may not originate in heaven, still go beyond our intent and our control, attaining with regard to the individual a sort of transcendence. Nor are poets and novelists the only ones to address this problem. Douglas Hofstadter, who studies the intellect, addresses it in his famous volume *Gödel, Escher, Bach,* in which the real problem is that of choosing among various images that have "rained" into the imagination.

> Think, for instance, of a writer who is trying to convey certain ideas which to him are contained in mental images. He isn't quite sure how those images fit together in his mind, and he experiments around, expressing things first one way and then another, and finally settles on some version. But does he know where it all came from? Only in a vague sense. Much of the source, like an iceberg, is deep underwater, unseen—and he knows that.

But perhaps we should first review the ways in which this problem has been framed in the past. The most thorough, lucid, and concise history of the idea of imagination that I've found is Jean Starobinski's essay "The Empire of the Imaginary" ("L'empire de l'imaginaire," from *La relation critique* [*The Critical Relation*], 1970). From Renaissance magic with its Neo-Platonic roots comes the notion of the imagination as a communicative link to the world soul, a notion later important to Romanticism and Surrealism. This contrasts with the idea of the imagination as a tool of knowledge, according to which the imagination, though it may take different routes than scientific knowledge, can nonetheless coexist and cooperate with it, can even be for the scientist a necessary stage in the formulation of his hypotheses. On the other hand, though they may accord with a Naturphilosophie or with a kind of theosophical knowledge, theories of the imagination as a repository for the truths of the universe are incompatible with scientific knowledge—unless we divide the knowable in two, leaving the outer world to science and confining imaginative knowledge to our individual inner lives. It is this latter position that Starobinski recognizes in the methods of Freudian analysis, while he links Jung's methods, which attribute universal validity to archetypes and to the collective unconscious, to the idea of the imagination as participation in the truth of the world.

At this point an unavoidable question arises: In which of the two currents described by Starobinski do I place my own idea of the imagination? To answer this question I must somehow retrace my experience as a writer, especially the part that involves my more "fantastic" narratives. When I began writing fantastic stories, I hadn't yet considered theoretical questions; the only thing I was certain of was that all of my stories originated with a visual image. One of these images, for example, was that of a man cut in two halves, each of which goes on living independently; another was a boy who climbs up a tree and travels from tree to tree without ever coming back down; yet another was an empty suit of armor that moves and speaks as if someone were inside it.

For me, then, the first step in the conception of a story occurs when an image that comes to mind seems, for whatever reason, charged with meaning, even if I can't explain that meaning in logical or analytical terms. As soon as the image has become clear enough in my mind, I begin developing it into a story, or rather the images themselves give rise to their own implicit potentialities, to the story they carry within them. Around each image others come into being, creating a field of analogies, symmetries, juxtapositions. At this point my shaping of this material—which is no longer purely visual but conceptual as well—begins to be guided by my intent to give order and sense to the story's progression. Or, to put it another way, what I'm doing is trying to establish which meanings are compatible with the general design I want to give the story and which are not, always allowing for a certain range of possible alternatives. At the same time, the writing, the verbal rendering, assumes ever-greater importance. I would say that as soon as I begin to put black on white, the written word begins to take over, first in an attempt to match the visual image, then as a cohesive development of the initial stylistic impulse, until little by little it rules the whole field. Then it is the writing that must guide the story toward its most felicitous verbal expression, and all that's left for the visual imagination is to keep up.

In *Cosmicomics* my process was a little different, because the point of departure was a conceptual statement drawn from scientific discourse, and it was from that that the free play of visual images had to arise. My intent was to demonstrate how the image-based discourse typical of myth could grow from any soil—even from a language, like that of today's science, that's as far from imagistic as can be. When reading even the most technical science or the most abstract philosophy, one may come across a phrase that unexpectedly spurs the figurative imagination. We thus find ourselves in one of those situations where the image is determined by a preexisting written text (a page or a single phrase I come across in my reading), and the resulting imaginative course might follow the spirit of that text or might take a completely independent path.

The first cosmicomic I wrote, "The Distance of the Moon," is also the most so to speak "surrealist," in the sense that the initial idea, based on gravitational physics, clears the way for a dreamlike fantasia. In other cosmicomics, the plot is driven by an idea that sticks closer to its scientific point of departure but that is always wrapped in a shell of images, of emotions, of monologuing or dialoguing voices.

In short, my method tries to join the spontaneous generation of images to the intentionality of logical thought. Even when the opening move is made by the visual imagination, operating according to its own intrinsic logic, it will sooner or later find itself caught in a web in which reasoning and verbal expression also impose their logic. And yet visual solutions remain crucial, sometimes showing up unexpectedly to decide situations that neither the surmises of thought nor the resources of language would be able to resolve.

A clarification regarding anthropomorphism in *Cosmicomics:* science interests me precisely because of my efforts to escape anthropomorphic knowledge; at the same time, however, I'm convinced that our imagination can only be anthropomorphic—and that's why I ventured to represent anthropomorphically a universe in which man has never existed, in which indeed it seems exceedingly unlikely that he ever could exist.

The time has come to answer the question I put to myself regarding the two currents identified by Starobinski: imagination as tool of knowledge or as identification with the world soul. Which do I claim? Going by what I was just saying, I ought to be a staunch supporter of the first tendency, since for me a story joins the spontaneous logic of images to a design guided by rational intent. At the same time, though, I've always looked to the imagination as a route to knowledge that lies beyond the individual, beyond the subjective; it would therefore be fair to declare myself closer to the second position: imagination as identification with world soul.

But there is another definition in which I recognize myself fully, and that is of the imagination as repertoire of the potential, of the hypothetical, of that which is not and has not been and may never be but could have been. In Starobinski's study, this view comes up in the discussion of Giordano Bruno. According to Bruno, the *spiritus phantasticus* is the "world or gulf, insatiable, of forms and images" (*mundus quidam et sinus inexplebilis formarum et specierum*). I believe, then, that it's crucial that every form of knowledge draw on this gulf of potential multiplicity. The mind of the poet and in certain key moments the mind of the scientist both function according to a process of image association, which is the quickest way to link and choose among the infinite forms of the possible and the impossible. The imagination is a kind of electronic machine that keeps track of all possible combinations and selects those that suit a particular purpose, or simply those that are the most interesting or pleasing or amusing.

I have yet to clarify the part played in this gulf of the imagination by the indirect imaginary, by which I mean the images provided by culture, whether mass culture or some other form. And that question implies another: What will the future of the individual imagination be in what is often called the "image civilization"? Will humanity's power to evoke images in absentia continue to develop as it is increasingly swamped by the flood of ready-made images? The visual memory of individuals used to be restricted to the legacy of their direct experience and to a limited repertoire of culturally reflected images; the opportunity to give shape to a personal myth arose from the way in which fragments of that memory could come together in surprising and suggestive ways. Nowadays we are bombarded by so many images that we can no longer distinguish direct experience from what we've seen for a few seconds on television. Bits of images cover our memory like a layer of trash, and among so many shapes it becomes ever more difficult for any one to stand out.

If I have included visibility in my list of qualities worth preserving, it is because we are in danger of losing a basic human faculty: the power to bring visions into focus with our eyes closed, to cause colors and shapes to spring forth from an array of black characters on a white page, to think through images. I have in mind a potential pedagogy of the imagination that would assist in the control of inner vision, that would neither suffocate it nor let it slip into vague, ephemeral fancy but would instead allow images to crystallize into forms that are distinct, memorable, autonomous — *icastic*.

Of course I'm describing a pedagogy that one can implement only upon oneself, with ad hoc methods and unpredictable results. My earliest formative experiences were already those of a child of the "image civilization," which was then, however, only in its infancy, far from the surfeit of today. I am the product, let's say, of an intermediate period, one in which the colorful illustrations of childhood — from books and children's weeklies and toys — mattered a great deal, and I think that being born in that time had a profound effect on my development. My imaginative world was shaped early on by the pictures in the *Corriere dei Piccoli*, at that time the most widely circulated children's weekly in Italy. I'm speaking of a time in my life that stretched from three to thirteen years of age, before the passion for movies that utterly possessed me for the whole of my adolescence. The crucial period, in fact, was probably from three to six, before I learned to read.

In the 1920s, the *Corriere dei Piccoli* published the most famous American comics of the time: *Happy Hooligan, The Katzenjammer Kids, Felix the Cat, Bringing Up Father*—all rechristened with Italian names. And there were Italian strips too, some of them outstanding in terms of their graphical taste and period style. Italy in those days had not yet begun to use dialogue balloons (those arrived in the thirties with the importation of Mickey Mouse). The *Corriere dei Piccoli* would redesign the American strips, eliminating the balloons and adding one or two rhymed couplets beneath each panel. Since I didn't know how to read anyway, I didn't miss the words at all—for me, the pictures were enough. I grew up with this little magazine, which my mother had begun buying and collecting before I was born, binding them into volumes by year. I would spend hours following each strip from one issue to the next, mentally recounting the stories with various interpretations of the scenes, coming up with alternate versions, fusing individual episodes into a broader story, discovering and isolating and connecting the recurring elements in each strip, mixing one strip with another, imagining new strips in which secondary characters became protagonists . . .

When I learned to read, the advantage gained was minimal. The silly rhyming couplets provided no useful information, and their interpretations of the stories were often as much shots in the dark as my own; it was clear that the versifiers had no idea what was written in the original balloons, either because they didn't know English or because they were working from strips that had already been redesigned and rendered mute. In any case I preferred to ignore the lines of text and carry on my favorite pastime of imagining from *within* the illustrations as they followed one upon the other.

This habit no doubt delayed my capacity for focusing on the written word (the attention necessary for reading was something I developed only later, and with effort), but for me reading the pictures without the words was undoubtedly an education in storytelling, stylization, and image composition. The graphical elegance, for example, of Pat Sullivan, who within a small square frame sets the black outline of Felix the Cat on a road that disappears into a landscape crowned by full moon in a black sky—I think that has remained an ideal for me.

The task I undertook as an adult in *Il castello dei destini incrociati* (*The Castle of Crossed Destinies,* 1973)—extracting stories from sequences of mysterious figures of the tarot, interpreting a particular figure in a different way each time—undoubtedly had its roots in my childish reveries over cartoon-filled pages. I was attempting in that book a kind of imaginary iconology, not only with the tarot but also with certain great paintings. In fact I tried to interpret the Carpaccios in San Giorgio degli Schiavoni in Venice by following the cycles of Saint George and Saint Jerome as if they were a single story, the life of one man, and identifying my own life with that of George/Jerome. This imaginary iconology became a habitual way for me to express my great love of painting: I adopted the technique of using famous pictures, or at least images that fascinated me, as starting points for telling my stories.

Let's say that various elements come together to form the visual part of the literary imagination: direct observation of the real world; phantasmal and oneiric transfiguration; the figurative world as transmitted by the culture at its various levels; and a process of abstraction, condensation, and interiorization of sensory experience, which is as crucial for visualizing as it is for verbalizing thought. All these elements are present to some degree in the authors I recognize as models, especially during those periods whose literatures were particularly rich in visual imagination: the Renaissance, the Baroque, and Romanticism. In an anthology I edited of nineteenth-century fantastic tales (*Racconti fantastici dell'Ottocento*), I followed the visionary and spectacular vein that leads from the stories of Hoffmann, Chamisso, Arnim, Eichendorff, Potocki, Gogol, Nerval, Gautier, Hawthorne, Poe, Dickens, Turgenev, and Leskov to those of Stevenson, Kipling, and Wells. And I also followed another vein, which runs parallel to the first and sometimes through the same authors, in which the fantastic springs from the commonplace —an internal, mental, invisible fantastic, which culminates in Henry James.

Will a literature of the fantastic be possible in the twenty-first century, considering the growing surfeit of ready-made images? At this point two directions seem possible. 1) We could recycle our used images in new contexts that alter their meaning. Postmodernism could be seen as the tendency to make ironic use of mass-media images, or else to introduce a taste for the marvelous inherited from the literary tradition into narrative mechanisms that accentuate its foreignness. 2) Or we could wipe the slate clean and start over from scratch. Samuel Beckett achieved the most extraordinary results by reducing visual and linguistic elements to the bare minimum, as if in a world after the end of the world.

Perhaps the first text in which all these problems coincided was Balzac's "Le Chef-d'oeuvre inconnu" ("The Unknown Masterpiece"). And it's no accident that an insight that might be seen as prophetic came from Balzac, who lived at a crossroads in literary history, in a "borderland" existence, now a visionary, now a realist, now both at once, always as if pulled along by forces of nature, but also always quite aware of what he was doing.

"Le Chef-d'oeuvre inconnu," on which he worked from 1831 to 1837, was originally called a "fantastic tale" (*conte fantastique*), while the definitive version appeared as a "philosophical study" (*étude philosophique*). In between, something happened: "literature," as Balzac himself declared in a different story, "killed the fantastic" (*la littérature a tué le fantastique*).

In the first version, published in a magazine in 1831, the old painter Frenhofer's perfect painting, in which a single female foot emerges from a chaos of color, from a shapeless fog, is understood and admired by two colleagues, François Porbus and Nicolas Poussin: "So many delights on this one bit of canvas!" (*Combien de jouissances sur ce morceau de toile!*) Even the model, who doesn't understand the painting, seems somehow impressed. In the second version (still in 1831 but in book form), some added remarks reveal the incomprehension of his colleagues. Frenhofer is still an enlightened mystic who lives for his ideal, but he is now condemned to solitude. The definitive version of 1837 adds a number of pages of technical reflections on painting and an ending that reveals that Frenhofer is a madman who ends up locking himself away with his supposed masterpiece, burning it and killing himself.

"Le Chef-d'oeuvre inconnu" has often been treated as a parable on the development of modern art. After reading the most recent such study, Hubert Damisch's *Fenêtre jaune cadmium* (*Cadmium Yellow Window,* 1984), I saw that the story could also be understood as a parable of literature, about the unbridgeable chasm between linguistic expression and sensory experience, about the slipperiness of the visual imagination. The first version of the story defines the fantastic as indefinable:

> *Pour toutes ces singularités, l'idiome moderne n'a qu'un*
> *mot:* c'etait indéfinissable! . . . *Admirable expression!*
> *elle résume la littérature fantastique; elle dit tout ce qui*

échappe aux perceptions bornées de notre esprit; et, quand vous l'avez placée sous les yeux d'un lecteur, il est lancé dans l'espace imaginaire.

For all these singularities, our modern idiom has but one phrase: *it was indefinable!* ... An admirable expression! It sums up the literature of the fantastic; it says everything that eludes the limited perceptions of our spirit; and when you place it beneath the eyes of a reader, he is launched into imaginary space.

In the years to come, Balzac rejects the literature of the fantastic, which for him has meant art as mystical knowledge of everything, and he undertakes the minute description of the world as it is, still convinced that he is expressing the secret of life. Just as he was for a long while unsure whether to make Frenhofer a seer or a madman, so his story retains an ambiguity in which its deepest truth resides. The artist's imagination is a world of potentialities that no single work will successfully enact; what we experience as we live is a different world, which answers to other forms of order and disorder; the layers of words that accumulate on pages like layers of color on canvas are yet another world, infinite too but more manageable, less resistant to forms. The relationship between these three worlds is that *indefinable* of which Balzac spoke—or let's call it, rather, *undecidable,* like the paradox of an infinite set that contains other infinite sets.

Writers—I mean writers of infinite ambition, like Balzac —perform operations that involve either the infinity of their imaginations or the infinity of realizable contingencies, or both, by means of the infinite linguistic possibilities of writing. Some may object that a single life, from birth to death, can contain only a finite quantity of information—how can the individual imagination and individual experience extend beyond that limit? Well, I think that these attempts to avoid the vertigo of the immeasurable are futile. Giordano Bruno explained that the *spiritus phantasticus* from which the writer's imagination draws forms and images is a bottomless well. And as for external reality, Balzac's *Comédie humaine* begins with the premise that the written world can be constructed in homology with the living world, today's as well as yesterday's and tomorrow's.

Balzac the fantasist tried to capture the world soul through a single figure among the infinite number imaginable, but in order to do so had to charge the written word, as the painter Frenhofer did his colors and lines, with such intensity that in the end it would no longer have referred to a world outside itself. Reaching that threshold, Balzac stopped and changed direction: he turned from intensive writing to extensive writing. Balzac the realist will attempt to cover with writing the infinite expanse of space and time, teeming with all its multitudes, its lives, its stories.

But couldn't things turn out the way they do in those Escher pictures that Douglas Hofstadter uses to illustrate Gödel's paradox? In a picture gallery, a man looks at a cityscape and the cityscape expands to include both the gallery that contains it and the man who is looking at it. In his infinite *Comédie humaine,* Balzac will have to include both the fantasist that he is or was, with all his infinite fantasies, and the realist that he is or wants to be, intent on capturing the infinite real world in his *Comédie humaine.* (Or perhaps it is the interior world of Balzac the fantasist that includes the interior world of Balzac the realist, because one of the infinite fantasies of the former coincides with the realistic infinity of the *Comédie humaine . . .*)

In any case, all "realities" and "fantasies" can take shape only through writing, in which exteriority and interiority, world and self, experience and imagination, are all composed of the same verbal material. The polymorphic visions of the eyes and the spirit find themselves embodied in uniform lines of lower- and uppercase letters, of periods and commas and parentheses. These pages of signs, as dense as grains of sand, represent the variegated spectacle of the world upon a surface that is always the same and always different, like dunes driven by the desert wind.

5

Multiplicity

Let's begin with a quotation:

Nella sua saggezza e nella sua povertà molisana, il dottor Ingravallo, che pareva vivere di silenzio e di sonno sotto la giungla nera di quella parrucca, lucida come pece e riccioluta come d'agnello d'Astrakan, nella sua saggezza interrompeva talora codesto sonno e silenzio per enunciare qualche teoretica idea (idea generale s'intende) sui casi degli uomini: e delle donne. A prima vista, cioè al primo udirle, sembravano banalità. Non erano banalità. Così quei rapidi enunciati, che facevano sulla sua bocca il crepitio improvviso d'uno zolfanello illuminatore, rivivevano poi nei timpani della gente a distanza di ore, o di mesi, dalla enunciazione: come dopo un misterioso tempo incubatorio. "Già!" riconosceva l'interessato: "il dottor Ingravallo me l'aveva pur detto". Sosteneva, fra l'altro, che le inopinate catastrofi non sono mai la conseguenza o l'effetto che dir si voglia d'un unico motivo, d'una causa al singolare: ma sono come un vortice, un punto di depressione ciclonica nella coscienza del mondo, verso cui hanno cospirato tutta una molteplicità di causali convergenti. Diceva anche nodo o groviglio, o garbuglio, o gnommero, che alla romana vuol dire gomitolo. Ma il termine giuridico "le causali, la causale" gli sfuggiva preferentemente di bocca: quasi contro sua voglia. L'opinione che bisognasse "riformare in noi il senso della categoria di causa" quale avevamo dai filosofi, da Aristotele o da Emmanuele Kant, e sostituire alla causa le cause era in lui una opinione centrale e persistente: una fissazione, quasi: che gli evaporava dalle labbra carnose, ma piuttosto bianche, dove un mozzicone di sigaretta spenta pareva, pencolando da un angolo, accompagnare la sonnolenza dello sguardo e il quasi-ghigno, tra amaro e scettico, a cui per "vecchia" abitudine soleva atteggiare la metà inferiore della faccia, sotto quel sonno della fronte e delle palpebre e quel nero pìceo della parrucca. Così, proprio così, avveniva dei "suoi" delitti. "Quanno me chiammeno! . . . Già. Si me chiammeno a me . . . può sta ssicure ch'è nu guaio: quacche gliuommero . . . de sberretà . . ." diceva, contaminando napolitano, molisano, e italiano.

La causale apparente, la causale principe, era sì, una. Ma il fattaccio era l'effetto di tutta una rosa di causali che gli eran soffiate addosso a molinello (come i sedici venti della rosa dei venti quando s'avviluppano a tromba in una depressione ciclonica) e avevano finito per strizzare nel vortice del delitto la debilitata "ragi-

one del mondo". Come si storce il collo a un pollo. E poi soleva dire, ma questo un po' stancamente, "ch'i' femmene se retroveno addo' n'i vuò truvà". Una tarda riedizione italica del vieto "cherchez la femme". E poi pareva pentirsi, come d'aver calunniato 'e femmene, e voler mutare idea. Ma allora si sarebbe andati nel difficile. Sicché taceva pensieroso, come temendo d'aver detto troppo. Voleva significare che un certo movente affettivo, un tanto o, direste oggi, un quanto di affettività, un certo "quanto di erotìa", si mescolava anche ai "casi d'interesse", ai delitti apparentemente più lontani dalle tempeste d'amore. Qualche collega un tantino invidioso delle sue trovate, qualche prete più edotto dei molti danni del secolo, alcuni subalterni, certi uscieri, i superiori, sostenevano che leggesse dei libri strani: da cui cavava tutte quelle parole che non vogliono dir nulla, o quasi nulla, ma servono come non altre ad accileccare gli sprovveduti, gli ignari. Erano questioni un po' da manicomio: una terminologia da medici dei matti. Per la pratica ci vuol altro! I fumi e le filosoficherie son da lasciare ai trattatisti: la pratica dei commissariati e della squadra mobile è tutt'un altro affare: ci vuole della gran pazienza, della gran carità: uno stomaco pur anche a posto: e, quando non traballi tutta la baracca dei taliani, senso di responsabilità e decisione sicura, moderazione civile; già: già: e polso fermo. Di queste obiezioni così giuste lui, don Ciccio, non se ne dava per inteso: seguitava a dormire in piedi, a filosofare a stomaco *vuoto, e a fingere di fumare la sua mezza sigheretta, regolarmente spenta.*

In his wisdom and in his Molisan poverty, Detective Ingravallo, who seemed to live on silence and sleep beneath the black jungle of that mop, as glossy as pitch and as curly as an astrakhan lamb—in his wisdom he sometimes interrupted that sleep and that silence to utter some theoretical notion (some general idea, I mean) on the nature of men . . . and women. At first glance, or rather on first hearing, they seemed like banalities. They were not banalities. And so it was that those abrupt utterances, which crackled from his lips like sulfur matches, sudden and illuminating, would come back to life in people's eardrums hours or even months later, as if after some mysterious period of incubation. "Of course!" the party in question would realize; "that's just what Detective Ingravallo told me." He would assert, among other things, that an unforeseen disaster is never the consequence or, if you prefer, the effect of a single factor, of only one cause, but rather is like a whirlwind, a point of cyclonic depression in the consciousness of the world, toward which a whole multiplicity of converging causalities have conspired. He'd also say knot or tangle or jumble—or *gnommero*, which in Roman dialect means a ball of yarn. But the legal term—*causalities, causality*—had a tendency to slip from his mouth as if against his will. The belief that we must "reform within ourselves the meaning of the category of cause" that philosophers from Aristotle to Kant had left us with, replacing cause with causes—this for him was a central and abiding belief, almost a fixation, that would waft from his fleshy but rather pallid lips, where the butt of a spent cigarette, dangling at one side, seemed to go with his somnolent gaze and that near-sneer, halfway between bitter and skeptical, that was stamped by "old" habit on the lower half of his face, beneath his sleepy brow and eyelids and that pitchy black mop of hair. That's how, precisely how, "his" crimes happened: "When they call on me! Yep. When they call on me . . . ya can bet there's trouble, some kinda snarl-up . . . to unscramble," he would say, mixing Neapolitan, Molisan, and Italian.

The apparent causality, the principal causality, was, in fact, single. But the misdeed was the result of a whole cluster of causalities that had buffeted it like a whirlwind (like the sixteen winds of the wind rose, twisting funnel-style into a cyclonic depression) until at last the vortex of the crime had tightened around the weakened "reason of the world." Like wringing a chicken's neck. And then he would add, a little wearily, "What with women turnin' up where ya don't wanna find 'em." A belated Italic reformulation of the stale "cherchez la femme." Then he'd seem to regret it, as if he had slandered women, and want to take it back. But that would have been a pain. So he brooded in silence, as if worried that he'd said too much. What he meant was that a certain emotional motive, a quantity or as they say these days a quantum of emotion, a certain "quantum of eros," got mixed up even in "crimes of interest," those that seemed far removed from the tempests of passion. A few colleagues, faintly jealous of his insights, a few priests, well versed in the many evils of our time, certain subalterns, some bailiffs, his supervisors — these claimed he read strange books, from which he gleaned all those words that had no meaning, or nearly none, yet were just the thing for bedazzling the greenhorns, the know-nothings. His arguments were mind-bending, his language that of loony-bin shrinks. No use in the real world! Better to leave snake oil and noodling to the treatise writers; actual police work down at the station or out in the field is something else entirely: it takes great patience, great compassion, and a strong stomach to boot—along with, at least when the

whole Italian rat trap isn't teetering on the brink,
a sense of responsibility and firm resolve, of civil
moderation—and yes, yes, a steady hand. But as
for these quite reasonable objections, he, Don Ciccio, paid them no mind: he went on sleeping on
his feet, philosophizing on an empty stomach, and
pretending to smoke his half-cigarette, which kept
going out.

The passage you've just heard is from the opening of Carlo
Emilio Gadda's novel *Quer pasticciaccio brutto de via Merulana*
(*That Nasty Mess on Merulana Street,* 1957). I wanted to begin
with this quotation because it seems quite well suited to introducing the subject of this talk, which is the contemporary
novel as encyclopedia, as method of knowledge, and above
all as network of connections among events, among people,
among the things of the world.

I could have chosen other authors to illustrate this tendency in novels of our century. I chose Gadda not only because he writes in my language and is relatively unknown in
the United States (in part because of the distinctive complexity of his style, difficult even in Italian), but also because his
philosophy lends itself quite well to my argument, in that
he sees the world as a "system of systems" in which each
individual system conditions the others and is conditioned by
them.

Carlo Emilio Gadda tried all his life to represent the world as a tangle or jumble or ball of yarn, to represent it without in any way diminishing the essential complexity of it or, to put it better, the simultaneous presence in it of very disparate elements that converge to determine each event.

He was led to this view of things by his intellectual training, his writerly temperament, and his neuroses. By training he was an engineer, shaped by scientific culture, technical expertise, and a genuine philosophical passion. This last remained, you might say, secret: the draft of a philosophical system inspired by Spinoza and Leibniz was discovered among his posthumous papers. As a writer, Gadda — considered something of an Italian Joyce — developed a style to match his complex epistemology, mixing various high and low linguistic levels and a wide variety of lexicons. As a neurotic, Gadda empties himself onto every page he writes, with all his anxieties and obsessions, often to the point of obscuring the overall design, as details proliferate to cover the whole canvas. What was meant to be a detective novel is left without a solution — and it can be said that all his novels have been left in the state of unfinished works or fragments, like the ruins of ambitious projects still marked by the splendor and the meticulous care with which they were conceived.

To consider how Gadda's encyclopedism can function in a finished work, we can turn to a shorter piece, such as, for example, his recipe "Risotto alla milanese," which is a masterpiece of Italian prose and practical wisdom thanks to its descriptions of rice grains still partly covered by their hulls (pericarps), of the most suitable pans, of saffron, and of the various stages of cooking. Another, similar text is devoted to construction technology, which, after the adoption of reinforced concrete and hollow bricks, no longer protects dwellings from either heat or noise; there follows a grotesque description of his life in a modern building and his obsession with all the noises of his neighbors that reach his ears.

In Gadda's shorter pieces, as in every episode of his novels, even the most minor of objects is seen as the center of a network of relations that the writer can't help but trace, causing details to multiply until his descriptions and digressions become endless. Regardless of the starting point, the scope broadens to include ever-greater horizons, and if it could keep expanding in every direction it would eventually encompass the entire universe.

The best example of these networks that radiate from every object is the episode from chapter 9 of *Quer pasticciaccio brutto de via Merulana* in which the stolen jewels are recovered. We get accounts of every precious stone — its geological history, its chemical composition, its artistic and historical connections, along with all its potential uses and the associated images they evoke. The definitive critical study of the epistemology implicit in Gadda's writing, Gian Carlo Roscioni's *La disarmonia prestabilita* (Preestablished disharmony), begins with an analysis of those five pages about jewels. From there Roscioni explains how for Gadda a knowledge of things as the convergences of "infinite relations, past and future, real or possible" (*infinite relazioni, passate e future, reali o possibili*), demands that everything be accurately named, described, and located in space and time. This is achieved by exploiting the semantic potential of words and the full range of verbal and syntactical forms, with their connotations and colorations and the often comedic effects produced by their juxtaposition.

Gadda's vision is characterized by grotesque comedy punctuated by frantic desperation. Even before science had officially ratified the principle that the act of observing somehow alters the observed phenomenon, Gadda knew that "to know is to insert something into the real and, therefore, deform the real" (*conoscere è inserire alcunché nel reale; è, quindi, deformare il reale*). From this arises his invariably deformative mode of representation and the tension he always generates between himself and the things he represents, such that the more the world is deformed beneath his gaze, the more the author's self is implicated in the process and is in turn deformed and deranged.

Passion for knowledge thus leads Gadda from the objectivity of the world to his own exasperated subjectivity, and this —for a man who doesn't like himself, indeed detests himself—is a terrifying ordeal, as he makes abundantly clear in his novel *La cognizione del dolore* (Knowledge of grief). In this book Gadda breaks into a wild invective against the pronoun *I*, indeed against all pronouns, those parasites of thought: "The I, the I! Vilest of all the pronouns! Pronouns! They're the lice of thought. When thought has lice, it scratches like anyone else who has lice . . . And under its nails, then . . . you find pronouns—personal pronouns" (*L'io, io!* . . . *il più lurido di tutti i pronomi!* . . . *I pronomi! Sono i pidocchi del pensiero. Quando il pensiero ha i pidocchi, si gratta come tutti quelli che hanno i pidocchi* . . . *e nelle unghie, allora* . . . *ci ritrova i pronomi* . . . *i pronomi di persona*).

If Gadda's writing is defined by this tension between rational exactitude and frenetic deformation, these being the foundations of every cognitive process, there was in the same period another writer, Robert Musil—also an engineer and also with a scientific and philosophical background—who expressed the tension between mathematical exactitude and the roughness of human affairs in a completely different manner: fluid, ironic, controlled. A mathematics of single solutions—that was Musil's dream.

> *Aber er hatte noch etwas auf der Zunge gehabt; etwas von mathematischen Aufgaben, die keine allgemeine Lösung zulassen, wohl aber Einzellösungen, durch deren Kombination man sich der allgemeinen Lösung nähert. Er hätte hinzufügen können, dass er die Aufgabe des menschlichen Lebens für eine solche ansah. Was man ein Zeitalter nennt-ohne zu wissen, ob man Jahrhunderte, Jahrtausende oder die Spanne zwischen*

Schule und Enkelkind darunter verstehen soll-dieser breite, ungeregelte Fluss von Zuständen würde dann ungefähr ebensoviel bedeuten wie ein planloses Nacheinander von ungenügenden und einzeln genommen falschen Lösungsversuchen, aus denen, erst wenn die Menschheit sie zusammenzufassen verstünde, die richtige und totale Lösung hervorgehen könnte.

In der Strassenbahn erinnerte er sich auf dem Heimweg daran.

But there was something else that he [Ulrich] had also had on the tip of his tongue, something about mathematical problems that did not admit of any general solution, though they did admit of particular solutions, the combining of which brought one nearer to the general solution. He might have added that he regarded the problem set by every human life as one of these. What one calls an age—without knowing whether one should by that understand centuries, millennia, or the span of time between schooldays and grandparenthood—this broad, unregulated flux of conditions would then amount to approximately as much as a chaotic succession of unsatisfactory and (when taken singly) false attempts at a solution, attempts that might produce the correct and total solution, but only when humanity had learnt to combine them all.

In the tram going home, he remembered this.

(trans. by Eithne Wilkins and Ernst Kaiser)

Knowledge, for Musil, is the awareness of the irrecon-cilability of two polarities: one he calls by turns exactitude, mathematics, pure spirit, or even military mentality; the other he calls soul, or irrationality, or humanity, or chaos. He puts everything he knows or thinks into an encyclopedic book, which he strives to maintain in the form of a novel though its structure keeps changing, coming apart in his hands, so that not only is he unable to finish the novel, but he can't even decide what general shape it should take in order to hold the vast quantity of material within clear borders. When contrasting these two engineer-writers—Gadda, for whom understanding meant letting himself be implicated in networks of relations, and Musil, who gives the impression of always understanding things in all their multiplicity of codes and levels without ever letting himself be implicated —we must also recognize a quality they shared: an inability to finish.

Proust too failed to finish his novel-encyclopedia, though not, clearly, for lack of a design, since the idea for *À la re-cherche du temps perdu* (*In Search of Lost Time*) came to him entire—the beginning and the end and the general shape— but rather because the work kept thickening and expanding from within, in accordance with its own vital processes. The network that links all things is Proust's theme as well, but for him the network consists of spatial-temporal points that are occupied in succession by every being, resulting in infinite multiplication of the dimensions of space and time. The world expands until it becomes ungraspable, and for Proust it is through the suffering of this ungraspability that we come to knowledge. In this sense, the jealousy inspired in the narrator by Albertine is a typical experience of knowledge:

> *Et je comprenais l'impossibilité où se heurte l'amour. Nous nous imaginons qu'il a pour objet un être qui peut être couché devant nous, enfermé dans un corps. Hélas! Il est l'extension de cet être à tous les points de l'espace et du temps que cet être a occupés et occupera. Si nous ne possédons pas son contact avec tel lieu, avec telle heure, nous ne le possédons pas. Or nous ne pouvons toucher tous ces points. Si encore ils nous étaient désignés, peut-être pourrions-nous nous étendre jusqu'à eux. Mais nous tâtonnons sans les trouver. De là la défiance, la jalousie, les persécutions. Nous perdons un temps précieux sur une piste absurde et nous passons sans le soupçonner à côté du vrai.*

And I understood the impossibility love comes up against. We imagine it has as its object a being that can be laid down before us, enclosed within a body. Alas! It is the extension of that being to every point of space and time that it has occupied or will occupy. If we do not possess its contact with a given place, a given hour, then we do not possess it. But we cannot touch all those points. If only they were marked for us, perhaps we could stretch out and reach them. But we grope without finding them. Hence mistrust, jealousy, paranoia. We waste precious time following an absurd trail and pass unsuspecting by the truth.

This passage is followed immediately by the one about the irascible deities that govern the telephone. A few pages later we witness an early demonstration of airplanes, and in the previous volume we saw automobiles take the place of carriages, changing the relationship of space to time to such a degree that "art is also changed by it" (*l'art en est aussi modifié*). I mention this to show that, compared with the engineer-writers I cited earlier, Proust was no slouch when it came to technological awareness. The advent of the technological modernity that we see gradually proliferate in *À la recherche du temps perdu* provides not merely "period color" but is part of the very form of the work, its internal logic, its eagerness to exhaust the multiplicity of the writable within the brief span of a life that is winding down.

I began my first talk with the poems of Lucretius and Ovid and with the model found in those two very different authors of a system of infinite relationships of all things with all things. In this talk I think that references to the literature of the past can be kept to a minimum—just enough to show how the literature of our time has taken on this ancient ambition to represent the multiplicity of relations, whether actual or potential.

Overly ambitious projects may be objectionable in many fields of endeavor, but not in literature. Literature can survive only by pursuing outsized goals, even those beyond all hope of achievement. Only if poets and writers set themselves tasks that no one else dares to imagine will literature continue to serve a purpose. As science begins to mistrust general explanations and solutions that are not narrow or specialized, the great challenge for literature will be to learn to weave together different kinds of knowledge and different codes into a pluralistic, multifaceted vision of the world.

One writer who clearly placed no limits on the ambitiousness of his projects was Goethe, who in 1780 confided to Charlotte von Stein that he was planning a "novel about the universe" (*Roman über das Weltall*). Little is known about how he intended to flesh out this idea, but his choice of the novel as the literary form capable of containing the whole universe is itself a fact charged with futurity. Around the same time, Lichtenberg wrote: "I believe that a poem about empty space could achieve great sublimity" (*Ich glaube, dass ein Gedicht auf den leeren Raum einer großen Erhabenheit fähig wäre*). The universe and the void: I'll return to these two terms, between which swings the aim of literature, and which often seem to mean the same thing.

I found these Goethe and Lichtenberg quotes in Hans Blumenberg's enthralling book *Die Lesbarkeit der Welt* (*The Legibility of the World,* 1979), in whose final chapters the author traces the history of this ambition from Novalis, who sought to write an "absolute book" that he sometimes saw as an encyclopedia and other times as a Bible, to Humboldt, who with his *Kosmos* completed his intended "physical description of the universe" (*physischen Weltbeschreibung*).

The chapter in Blumenberg that is most relevant to my theme is the one called "Das leere Weltbuch" ("The Empty Book of the World"), which concerns Mallarmé and Flaubert. I've always been fascinated by the fact that Mallarmé, who in his poetry managed to give nothingness an incomparably crystalline form, devoted the last years of his life to the task of an "absolute book" that would be the ultimate end of the universe — a mysterious work of which he destroyed every trace. I'm also fascinated to think that Flaubert, who on January 16, 1852, wrote to Louise Colet that "what I'd like to do is a book about nothing" (*ce que je voudrais faire, c'est un livre sur rien*), devoted the last decade of his life to the most encyclopedic novel ever written, *Bouvard et Pécuchet.*

Bouvard et Pécuchet is of course the true progenitor of the novels I'm discussing this evening, even if the pathetic and hilarious voyage on the seas of universal knowledge taken by those two Quixotes of nineteenth-century scientism leads to a series of shipwrecks. For this pair of naive autodidacts, every book opens a world, but the worlds are mutually exclusive or so contradictory as to destroy any hope of certainty. Despite their best efforts, the two scriveners lack that subjective gift that allows ideas to be adapted to desired ends or gratuitous pleasure to be taken from them—a talent that can't after all be learned from books.

But how should we understand the ending of this unfinished novel, with Bouvard and Pécuchet giving up on understanding the world, becoming resigned to the lot of scriveners, and deciding to dedicate themselves to copying the books of the universal library? Must we conclude that, in their experience, "encyclopedia" and "nothingness" fuse together? But behind the two characters stands Flaubert, who in order to feed their adventures chapter by chapter must build up his own expertise in every branch of learning, erecting an edifice of science for his two heroes to knock down. So he reads handbooks on agriculture and horticulture, chemistry, anatomy, medicine, geology . . . In a letter from August of 1873, he claims that for this purpose he has read (and taken notes on) 194 volumes; by June of 1874 this number has risen to 294; five years later he tells Zola, "I'm done with my readings and won't crack another book until my novel is finished" (*Mes lectures sont finies et je n'ouvre plus aucun bouquin jusqu'à la terminaison de mon roman*). But a little later, in other letters, we find him grappling with ecclesiastical texts, and then he studies pedagogy, which in turn requires him to fan out into a wide miscellany of other disciplines. In January of 1880 he writes: "Do you know how many volumes I've had to soak up for my two fine fellows? More than 1500!" (*Savez-vous à combien se montent les volumes qu'il m'a fallu absorber pour mes deux bonhommes? A plus de 1500!*)

The encyclopedic epic of the two autodidacts is therefore *doublée* by a mammoth parallel venture undertaken in real life: it is Flaubert himself who is being transformed into a universal encyclopedia, assimilating with a passion matching that of his heroes all the knowledge they seek to possess as well as all that will be denied them. Did he toil so long to illustrate the pointlessness of knowledge as it is used by his two autodidacts? (According to a letter from December 16, 1879, Flaubert wanted to subtitle the novel "On the lack of method in the sciences" [*Du défaut de méthode dans les sciences*]). Or the pointlessness of knowledge in general?

A century later another encyclopedic novelist, Raymond Queneau, wrote an essay defending the two heroes from the charge of stupidity—their downfall was being "besotted with the absolute" (*épris d'absolu*) and not allowing for contradiction or doubt—and defending Flaubert from the simplistic charge that he was opposed to science. Queneau writes: "Flaubert is *for* science precisely insofar as science is skeptical, reserved, methodical, cautious, humane. He has a horror of dogmatists, metaphysicians, and philosophers" (*Flaubert est pour la science dans la mesure justement où celle-ci est sceptique, réservée, méthodique, prudente, humaine. Il a horreur des dogmatiques, des métaphysiciens, des philosophes*).

Flaubert's skepticism and his boundless curiosity about the storehouse of human knowledge are the qualities that would be appropriated by the greatest writers of the twentieth century. But in their case I would speak of an active skepticism, of a sense of play and risk, in their dogged attempt to establish relations among discourses and methods and levels. Knowledge as multiplicity is the thread that links the major works both of so-called modernism and of so-called postmodernism — a thread that, labels aside, I hope will go on unspooling into the next millennium.

Let's remember that the book that is arguably the most comprehensive introduction to the culture of our century is a novel: Thomas Mann's *Der Zauberberg* (*The Magic Mountain*, 1924). It could be said that all the threads that were to be pursued by the century's *maîtres à penser* originated in the closed-off world of that Alpine sanatorium — all the subjects that to this day fuel debate were anticipated and reviewed there.

What develops in the great novels of the twentieth century is the idea of an *open encyclopedia* — and here the adjective of course contradicts the noun, which derives etymologically from the presumption that all the world's knowledge could be gathered and enclosed in a circle. Now any totality that is not potential, speculative, or plural is no longer thinkable.

If medieval literature tended toward works that assimilated human knowledge into stable, compact, ordered forms — works such as the *Divine Comedy*, where multifarious linguistic riches meet the application of systematic and unified thinking — the best-loved modern books, by contrast, arise from the confluence and collision of a multiplicity of interpretive methods, modes of thought, and styles of expression. Even if a work's overall design has been meticulously planned, what counts is not its enclosure within a harmonious shape but rather the centrifugal force it releases, with its multiplicity of languages as guarantee of a truth that isn't partial. This is illustrated by the two great writers of the century who were most rooted in the Middle Ages, Eliot and Joyce, both devotees of Dante and both with a deep understanding of theology (though with different intentions). Eliot dissolves his theological design in the lightness of irony and the dizzying spell of his language. Joyce fully intends to construct a systematic encyclopedic work that can be read on multiple levels according to medieval hermeneutics (he even compiles tables showing how the chapters of *Ulysses* correspond to parts of the human body, the arts, colors, and symbols), but it is above all an encyclopedia of styles that he achieves—chapter by chapter in *Ulysses* or through the polyphonic multiplicity of the verbal fabric in *Finnegans Wake*.

It's time to impose a little order on all the examples of multiplicity I've been gathering as I go.

There is the unified text that unfolds as the discourse of a single voice but that turns out to be interpretable on various levels. Here the prize for inventiveness and bravura goes to Alfred Jarry for *L'amour absolu* (*Absolute Love*, 1899), a fifty-page novel that can be read as three completely different stories: 1) the vigil of a condemned man in his cell on the eve of his execution; 2) the monologue of an insomniac who while half-asleep dreams of being condemned to death; and 3) the story of Christ.

There is the plural text, which replaces the uniqueness of the thinking "I" with a multiplicity of subjects, voices, and perspectives on the world, following the model that Mikhail Bakhtin called "dialogic" or "polyphonic" or "carnivalesque," and whose antecedents he traced from Plato through Rabelais to Dostoyevsky.

There is the work that in its eagerness to contain the whole of the possible fails to give itself a shape or define its own limits, and that remains incomplete thanks to the very mission that brought it into being, as we have seen with Musil and Gadda.

There is the work that is the literary equivalent of what in philosophy is called nonsystematic thought, which proceeds aphoristically, in irregular, dotlike flashes—and now the moment has come to cite an author I never tire of reading, Paul Valéry. I'm speaking of his prose work: essays of a few pages, notes of a few lines from his *Cahiers*. "A philosophy should be portable" (*Une philosophie doit être portative;* XXIV, 713), he wrote, but also "I have sought, am seeking, and will seek what I call the Total Phenomenon, that is to say the All of consciousness, relations, conditions, possibilities, impossibilities" (*J'ai cherché, je cherche et chercherai pour ce que je nomme le Phénomène Total, c'est à dire le Tout de la conscience, des relations, des conditions, des possibilités, des impossibilités;* XII, 722).

Among the qualities I would like to see passed down to

and embraced by the literature of the next millennium, this one is foremost: a taste for exactitude and intellectual order in which the intelligence of poetry joins that of science and philosophy, as it does in Valéry's prose. (And if I mention Valéry in a context dominated by the names of fiction writers, it is also because, though not a novelist himself — indeed, thanks to a famous quip of his, he was seen as the assassin of traditional fiction — he was a critic who understood novels like no one else, indeed defined specifically what made them novels.)

If I had to name a fiction writer who has perfectly realized Valéry's aesthetic ideal of imaginative and linguistic exactitude, creating works that respond to the rigorous geometry of the crystal and the abstraction of a deductive argument, I would without hesitation say Jorge Luis Borges. The reasons for my fondness of Borges don't end there. I'll try to list the most important: because every text of his contains a model of the universe or of an attribute of the universe: the infinite, the innumerable, time that is eternal or simultaneous or cyclical; because all these texts take up only a few pages, with an exemplary economy of expression; because often his stories take on the forms of some genre of popular literature, forms tested by long usage, which has turned them into almost mythic structures. For example, his most dizzying piece about time, "El jardín de los senderos que se bifurcan" ("The Garden of Forking Paths"), is presented as a spy story, which contains a story of logic and metaphysics, which in turn contains the description of an endless Chinese novel—all of this condensed into a dozen pages.

The hypotheses Borges advances in this story, each of which is contained (almost concealed) in a few lines, are these: the idea of "punctual" time, one that might be called an absolute subjective present: "I reflected that everything happens to everyone precisely, precisely now. Centuries upon centuries, and only in the present do things occur; innumerable men in the air, on land, and at sea, and everything that actually happens happens to me" (*reflexioné que todas las cosas le suceden a uno precisamente, precisamente ahora. Siglos de siglos y sólo en el presente ocurren los hechos; innumerables hombres en el aire, en la tierra y el mar y todo lo que realmente pasa me pasa a mi*); then the idea of time determined by will, in which the future appears as irrevocable as the past; and finally the story's central idea, a multiple, ramified time in which every present forks into two futures, so as to form "a growing, dizzying network of diverging, converging, and parallel times" (*una red creciente y vertiginosa de tiempos divergentes, convergentes y paralelos*). This idea of infinite simultaneous universes in which all possibilities are realized in all their possible combinations isn't a digression from the story but rather the very reason the protagonist allows himself to commit the absurd, despicable crime his spy mission demands of him: he knows it's happening only in one universe and not in the others, knows indeed that by committing the murder here and now, he and his victim may, in the other universes, greet each other as friends and comrades.

This model of a network of possibilities can therefore be condensed into a few pages of a Borges story, or it can serve as a load-bearing structure for long, even extremely long novels, in which the density of concentration is reproduced in the individual parts. But I would say that today the rule "Be Brief" is confirmed even by long novels, whose structures often seem cumulative, modular, and combinatory.

These considerations are for me at the root of what I call the "hyper-novel," of which I tried to offer an example with *Se una notte d'inverno un viaggiatore* (*If on a winter's night a traveler*, 1979). My goal was to give the essence of the novelistic, but condensed into ten beginnings, which develop in very different ways from a common nucleus and which act upon a frame story that both determines them and is determined by them. The same principle, that of sampling the potential multiplicity of what can be narrated, is at the root of another book of mine, *The Castle of Crossed Destinies*, which is meant to be a kind of machine for multiplying narratives, using as starting points images with various possible meanings, like those on tarot cards. My temperament leads me to "be brief," and these structures allow me to join density of invention and expression with a sense of infinite possibilities.

Another example of what I call the "hyper-novel" is Georges Perec's *La Vie mode d'emploi* (*Life a User's Manual*). A

very long novel, constructed of many stories that intersect
—it's not for nothing that its subtitle is *romans,* in the plural—it reawakens the pleasure of the great novel cycles à la
Balzac. In my view this book, published in Paris in 1978, four
years before the author's death at only forty-six, was the last
real event in the history of the novel. For many reasons: its
boundless yet complete design, its formal novelty, its précis
of a narrative tradition and its encyclopedic synthesis of different kinds of knowledge that give shape to an image of the
world, its feeling of the here and now which is partly created
by the accretion of the past and the vertigo of the void, its
continuous fusion of irony and anguish—in short, the way
in which the pursuit of a structural plan and the indeterminacy of poetry become one and the same.

The jigsaw puzzle lends the novel both a plot line and a
formal model. Another model is the cutaway view of a typical Parisian apartment block, whose ten floors provide the
setting for all the action. There is one chapter per room, and
for each we learn about the furniture and decor, the changes
of ownership, and the lives of the residents and even those of
their ancestors and descendants. The building plan functions
as a ten-by-ten grid: a chessboard on which Perec moves from
one square (i.e., room; i.e., chapter) to another, as a knight
moves, according to a certain pattern that enables it to land
on each square once. (So are there a hundred chapters? No,
there are ninety-nine—this ultra-finished book intentionally
gives us a glimpse of unfinishedness.)

All that is what we might call the container. As for what it contains, Perec drew up lists of subjects broken down into categories and decided that one subject from each category must appear (even if only in passing) in each chapter, with their combinations constantly varied according to mathematical procedures I can't define but whose exactitude I don't doubt. (I saw Perec often during the nine years he spent writing the novel, but I know only a few of his secret rules.) There are no fewer than forty-two of these categories, which include literary quotes, geographic locations, historical dates, furniture, objects, styles, colors, foods, animals, plants, minerals, and I don't know what else—nor do I know how he managed to follow all these rules in even the briefest chapters.

In order to escape the arbitrary nature of existence, Perec must, like his protagonist, submit to rigorous rules (even if these rules are in turn arbitrary). But the miracle is that this poetics, which might seem artificial and mechanical, results in inexhaustible freedom and richness of invention. This is because it coincides with his passion, evident since the appearance of his first novel, *Les choses* (*Things*, 1965), for catalogs: for lists of objects, each defined on its own terms and in relation to a period, a style, a society, and so forth—menus, concert programs, diet charts, real or imaginary bibliographies . . .

The demon of "collectionism" always hovers over the pages of Perec, and the collection that seems most "his" among the many that the book evokes is that of the *unicum* —the object, that is, of which only a single specimen exists. But in fact he was not, in his life, a collector, except of words, ideas, and memories. Terminological exactitude was his way of possessing things; he gathered and named whatever was unique about each incident and person and thing. No one was more immune than Perec to the worst plague of contemporary writing: vagueness.

I wish to stress the fact that for Perec, constructing his novel according to fixed rules or "constraints" stimulated rather than stifled narrative freedom. It's no accident that Perec was the most inventive member of the Oulipo, that "workshop of potential literature" (*ouvroir de littérature potentielle*) founded by his mentor, Raymond Queneau. It was Queneau who, many years earlier, in the days of his quarrel with the "automatic writing" of the surrealists, wrote:

> *Une autre bien fausse idée qui a également cours actuellement, c'est l'équivalence que l'on établit entre inspiration, exploration du subconscient et libération, entre hasard, automatisme et liberté. Or, cette inspiration qui consiste à obéir aveuglément à toute impulsion est en réalité un esclavage. Le classique qui écrit sa tragédie en observant un certain nombre de règles qu'il connaît est plus libre que le poète qui écrit ce qui lui passe par la tête et qui est l'esclave d'autres règles qu'il ignore.*
>
> (from *Bâtons, chiffres et lettres*, 1950)

Another quite false idea that is also widespread at the moment is the tendency to equate inspiration, exploration of the subconscious, and liberation; chance, automatism, and freedom. Now, *this* inspiration, which consists in blindly obeying every impulse, is in reality a kind of slavery. The classical author who in writing his tragedy follows a certain number of familiar rules is freer than the poet who writes down whatever comes into his head and who is a slave to other rules of which he is unaware.

(from *Sticks, Numbers, and Letters*, 1950)

I have now come to the end of my defense of the novel as a great network. Some may contend that the more a work tends toward the multiplication of possibilities, the further it drifts from that *unicum* that is the writer's self, from sincerity, from the discovery of personal truth. I would reply: On the contrary, for who are we, who is each of us, if not a combinatorics of experiences, of information, of things we have read and imagined? Every life is an encyclopedia, a library, an inventory of objects, a pattern book of styles, in which everything can be constantly remixed and rearranged in every possible fashion. And I have another reply, one that may be closer to my heart: what if it were possible for a work to be conceived beyond the self, a work that allowed us to escape the limited perspective of the individual ego, not only in order to enter other similar selves but to give voice to that which cannot speak—the bird perched on the gutter, the tree in spring and the tree in autumn, stone, cement, plastic . . .

Wasn't this, perhaps, where Ovid was going when he described the continuity of forms, where Lucretius was going when he identified himself with the nature that all things have in common?

Translator's Note

As current residents of the "next millennium," we are part of the future audience Calvino intended to address. The values he recommends to us in these pages have remained as essential, and arguably as endangered, as he no doubt guessed they would be, and it is my hope that this new translation will help bring them and his brilliant defenses of them to the attention of a new generation of readers and writers.

New translations rarely need justification, particularly after three decades have passed—translations date, after all, and multiple translations are nearly always in a work's best interest. But I would like briefly to explain how this one came to be. The 1988 translation, while serviceable, suffered from minor inaccuracies and other infelicities that I have tried to address. It also suffered, through no fault of the translator, from the fact that the author died prematurely, before he could edit the lectures for publication. With that in mind, and in consultation with Calvino's daughter, Giovanna Calvino, I have, in addition to retranslating them, edited them very lightly, in accordance with what we believe Calvino himself would have done had he had the chance. For example, at one point he slips and refers to the setting of Perec's *Life a User's Manual* as a five-story building, when in fact it is — as Calvino well knew — a ten-story building. In such cases, which were extremely rare, I have made silent corrections. And in one case (near the beginning of "Visibility") I have added a few words of transition before and after his gloss of a Dante passage. I have tried throughout to be guided by the very qualities Calvino here promotes: *lightness, quickness, visibility, exactitude* . . .

This retranslation began life in an unusual way, as an experiment in collaboration, primarily pedagogical in its ambitions, and I would like to acknowledge and thank those who conceived and participated in that experiment. The European Society of Authors, a nonprofit based in Paris, created a software platform called TLHUB (Translation and Literary Hub) designed to facilitate collaborative, web-based translation projects. Project leaders Jill McCoy and Camille Bloomfield chose Calvino's "memos" as a sort of pilot text. A team at the University of Chicago (led by Jennifer Scappettone) worked on "Quickness," a team at the University of Pennsylvania (led by Marina della Putta Johnston) worked on "Exactitude," a team at DePaul University (led by Caterina Mongiat-Farina) worked on "Visibility," a team at Pace University (led by Julia Heim) worked on "Multiplicity," and my own team at the University of Arkansas worked on "Lightness." Each team was free to choose its own working method; we divided "Lightness" into four parts, each of us translating one. But when we put the parts together and began to revise them collaboratively using TLHUB's online software, two things became clear: how distinct from one another our four parts were, in terms of tone and style, and how difficult it was to impose upon them, retroactively, tonal and stylistic consistency. While the project was successful from a pedagogical point of view, it took us longer to produce a single semi-cohesive version of "Lightness" than it would have taken us to produce four separate (and more cohesive) versions. Various phrases came to mind: too many cooks, design by committee, etc. But I think the fault here lay with our particular approach to collaboration rather than collaboration per se, and I continue to regard TLHUB as a promising platform.

It might have been illuminating to present these five essays in the translations done by the five groups; such a collection could have been offered in the spirit of the fifth memo, "Multiplicity." For the published version, however, we abandoned the collaborative model — guided instead, perhaps, by the unwritten sixth memo, "Consistency" — and I reworked "Lightness" and translated the other four essays myself. I benefited, as any retranslator does, from access to the original translation, and with regard to "Lightness" I also benefited from the insights of my graduate students, Anne Greeott, Christopher Tamigi, and Kathleen Heil — all outstanding translators in their own rights.

Finally I would like to thank Giovanna Calvino, for her guidance of this project and for her intelligent and passionate advocacy on behalf of her father's extraordinary legacy.